D0850780

The Rise of
ROMANCE

I. A KNIGHT RIDING IN SEARCH OF ADVENTURE (Sala del Consiglio, Palazzo Comunale, San Gimignano)

Photograph Mansell Collection

The Rise of

ROMANCE

BY

EUGÈNE VINAVER

D. S. BREWER

BARNES & NOBLE

Burgess

PQ
207
.V5
1984
C.1

© EUGÈNE VINAVER 1971

First published 1971

Reissued 1984 by
D. S. Brewer
240 Hills Road, Cambridge
an imprint of Boydell & Brewer Ltd
PO Box 9, Woodbridge, Suffolk IP12 3DF
and by
Barnes and Noble Books
81 Adams Drive, Totowa, New Jersey 07512

ISBN 0 85991 158 6
US ISBN 0-389-20449-8

Printed in Great Britain by
St Edmundsbury Press, Bury St Edmunds, Suffolk

FOR
HUGH VAUDREY

PREFACE

THE purpose of this work is to explore the early development of a literary form which is the foundation of narrative literature in the modern sense. If it does not claim to be a study of the 'origins' of the modern novel, it is not only because any such claim would in this instance be extravagant, but because the term 'origins' is generally inapplicable to literary forms. 'Humanity', as C. S. Lewis once told us, 'does not pass through phases as a train passes through stations: being alive, it has the privilege of always moving, yet never leaving anything behind.' Form in art and literature enjoys the same privilege; whatever it has been, in some sort it still is; not, of course, the form thought out by theorists, but the form which springs to life when the matter of a poem or a prose work is crystallized into a verbal structure, sounds into patterns of sound and light into colour and shape.

Some such forms cut across the most sharply defined historical and national boundaries, affirming the existence of creative processes mysteriously linked together regardless of their sequence in time or their distance from one another in space. The statue of Adam at Saint-Denis and those of the saints at Notre-Dame recall some of the shining examples of the art of Praxiteles, as if across the gulf of centuries the sun of Greece had touched the cathedrals of France. Literature offers striking parallels to such correspondences, and E. M. Forster, in an effort to generalize them, has even imagined 'all novelists writing their novels at once, no matter what ages and races they come from'—all at work 'together in a circular room'. Yet the energy which makes great novelists enter what he calls their 'common state' usually finds expression in less fortuitous encounters. To make the image of the circular room true to facts one would have to allow the novelists to move about in it and, without necessarily looking over each other's shoulder, share in certain changing varieties of formal vision. A critic observing the scene could then speculate with profit about the trends and currents within the circular room.

He would see it as a spacious playground of the 'shaping spirit of Imagination'—as an ever-expanding panorama of forms, now growing and spreading, now contracting and giving way to others endowed with equal powers. For this changing scene with its recurrences and contrasts, its inconsistencies and continuities, is the true matter of literary history, ignored though it is by most literary historians who assume for no apparent reason that ideas have both a past and a present, while art is either modern or old. Few of them have ever caught a glimpse of the scene, fewer still have grasped its significance. Walter Pater saw it perhaps in his mind's eye when he spoke of the 'House Beautiful' which 'the creative minds of all generations are always building together', resolving the age-long antinomy between the heritage that nothing can replace and the urge to build again; and the same vision must have been in Goethe's mind when he was ascending the steps of Strassburg cathedral, conscious with each step of a growing feeling for 'relationships, proportions and seemliness', which had caused man 'to build and to re-build at one and the same time'.

To come closer to this vast perspective and see how it affects narrative art, it is best to reflect not upon generalities but upon the few examples of that art which the accident of reading has brought to one's notice. The following pages are an experiment in this approach. Some of them have already appeared elsewhere under different headings[1] and are reproduced here, sometimes with substantial modifications, by permission of the publishers concerned; the bulk of the work, however, is based upon a series of lectures delivered as long ago as 1958 at Aberystwyth under

[1] These include extracts from three articles published in the *Bulletin of the John Rylands Library* (vol. xxxvi, pp. 228–44, vol. xl, pp. 515–26, and vol. xlvi, pp. 476–503), an article published in vol. xxv of *Medium Ævum* (pp. 175–80), two editions of texts (*Le Roman de Balain* (Manchester 1942), and Malory's *Tale of the Death of King Arthur* (Oxford 1955)), and the 1966 Presidential Address of the Modern Humanities Research Association (*Form and Meaning in Medieval Romance*). There is also much common ground, especially in the middle chapters (iii–v), between the present work and my recently published study entitled *A la Recherche d'une poétique médiévale* (Paris, Nizet). For permission to reprint the extracts my thanks are due to the John Rylands Library, the Manchester University Press, Messrs. B. H. Blackwell, the Clarendon Press, and the Modern Humanities Research Association.

the auspices of the Gregynog Foundation. To the authorities of
the University College of Wales, and especially to the then Principal
of the College and Professor E. R. Briggs, I am indebted not only
for the privilege of serving under this great foundation, but for
the opportunity they gave me of addressing an audience at once
appreciative and enlightened. The incentive to embark upon the
perilous, yet necessary, task of turning what was intended to be
spoken into something written was but one of the many benefits
I derived from a memorable week spent at a noble place of
learning.

On a later occasion, while I was still engaged upon this task,
I had the great good fortune to give a more extended course of
lectures on similar topics at the University of Chicago—an inspiring and enriching experience, as stimulating as any that I have
ever had with university audiences. Nor was I less lucky in the
choice of my first readers, John Steinbeck and C. S. Lewis. Neither
of them lived to see the work completed, but their friendly scrutiny
of one of its first drafts was to me at once spur and bridle, no
less irreplaceable than the impulse received from their own writings. Finally, in the last stages of this unduly long process of
preparation the Institute for Research in the Humanities at the
University of Wisconsin provided me with all the material facilities
and the intellectual stimulus I needed. Of the latter I had more
than my share thanks to my colleagues at the Institute, Professors
Germaine Brée, Julian Harris, Frank Horlbeck, James John,
Gwynn McPeek, Friedrich Solmsen, and Julius Weinberg.

My other debts cannot be quite so precisely dated. Before I
knew that I was going to write this book I was inspired to work on
something like it by the lifelong friend to whom it is dedicated
and who, I know, will not object if I couple his name with that of
another, still earlier, companion. It was through my repeated
efforts to understand the mind and art of Sir Thomas Malory that
the creative endeavours of his French predecessors—the initial
founders of romance in Europe—first appeared to me in their true
light: not as reflections of some imaginary *Temple du goût*, but as
significant events in the long and complex life of literary forms. It
may well be that the exact nature of these events still eludes us; but

if it does, a study such as this might at least point to their existence, and by the same token show how much of what is vital to our understanding of literary history in the true sense still lies beyond our grasp.

E. V.

December 1969

CONTENTS

LIST OF PLATES

I

ROLAND AT RONCEVAUX

IN the third quarter of the twelfth century, some ten or fifteen years after the disaster of the Second Crusade, a remarkable event occurred on the European literary scene. W. P. Ker describes it as something 'quite as momentous and far-reaching in its consequences as that to which the name "Renaissance" is generally appropriated'.[1] A series of French verse romances produced at that time established a new literary genre which, together with the influence of early Provençal lyric poetry, 'determined', as the same critic puts it, 'the forms of modern literature long after the close of the Middle Ages'. The tradition that preceded these romances, that of the heroic epic, had for nearly a century inspired the poets writing in the *langue d'oïl*. The romance writers turned away from it and at first borrowed their subjects from the legends of classical antiquity; but soon they discovered the realm of Arthurian knighthood—not the pseudo-historical kingdom of the chronicles of Geoffrey of Monmouth and Wace, but the imaginary land of pure chivalry whose fame rested on the exploits of King Arthur's knights. Love interest and the pursuit of adventures unrelated to any common aim thus displaced the theme of the defence of Christendom and the preoccupation with feudal warfare; and the new genre, breaking decisively with all varieties of the old epic tradition, made the division between the heroic and the chivalric age.

It is in some such terms that the change from epic to romance is usually described. But to leave it at that would be unenterprising if not unrealistic. One is tempted to wonder, on purely *a priori* grounds, whether any great change in literary history could ever have been caused by a simple transference of attention from one type of subject to another. What distinguishes one literary generation or one epoch from another is surely not the

---

[1] *Epic and Romance*, p. 323.

stories people tell but the way they tell them. If the advent of romance deserves to be called a momentous event, if it is true that even what is conventionally called 'the end of the Middle Ages' made no such abrupt change of outlook, then the nature and the meaning of the process must be related to some of the deeper undercurrents of our literary civilization. Ernst Curtius rightly remarks that in this as in other fields the significant facts are the least visible ones: like lodes in the rock, 'they lie hidden in the object and are "divined"—more properly, "tracked down"—by the seeker's dowsing rod'.[1] To the modern eye the 'rock' looks exasperatingly ordinary, and the modern reader's dowsing rod wanders hopelessly along its smooth surface.

An interesting attempt has recently been made to explain the event by reference to the 'spirit of the time'. R. W. Southern, in a remarkably well-documented chapter of his *Making of the Middle Ages*,[2] suggests that the transition from epic to romance was a reflection of the great social, intellectual, and spiritual change which had affected both the secular and the religious life of twelfth-century Europe. The change was exemplified in the teaching of St. Anselm and St. Bernard, in the shifting of emphasis from communal exercise in endurance to a view of life as 'individual seeking and journeying'; from a life where man 'was lost in the crowd and stripped of those eccentricities which we call his personality' to the spiritual growth of the individual, who orders his experiences consciously in a newly discovered area of freedom. St. Anselm's programme of spiritual life in solitude, in the company of a few chosen disciples, St. Bernard's view that man must know himself and 'by progress of self-knowledge ascend to the knowledge of God', are, according to Southern, examples of the inward quest which, on the secular plane, found expression in 'stories of the heart in search of love' and the 'adventures of the heart' so characteristic of the romances of Chrétien de Troyes.

In the knights of Arthur, [he writes] as in those of Charlemagne, there is a great sense of common objective, but it is a wholly ideal ob-

[1] Ernst Robert Curtius, *Europäische Literatur und lateinisches Mittelalter* (Bern, 1948), 387. English translation by W. R. Trask (p. 383).
[2] London, 1953, pp. 219–57.

jective, at once quite universal and quite individual. It is unthinkable
that the knights of the *Song of Roland* should fight each other without
a breach of their fundamental code of conduct: their ties of loyalty
and vassalage were too serious for that. They fight as members of a
body. However much a Roland may stand above his fellows in
prowess, he takes part in a common action against a common
enemy... The knights of Chrétien seek the enemy in solitude and in
the course of their search they may well find themselves striving
against one of their fellow-knights. There was nothing disconcerting
in this, for action was only a means to a spiritual end.[1]

It is, of course, true that the heroes of romance 'seek solitude
for the exercise of their essential virtue', much in the same way
as the Cistercians did; but it is also true that in Old French literature this solitary quest was not a prerogative of romance: it
existed in such works as *The Life of St. Alexis* and *The Voyage of
St. Brendan*, as well as some of the epics. To say that epic heroes
were 'circumscribed by their ties of lordship and vassalage and
by the sacred bond of comradeship' is to single out one of the
features which may seem to distinguish them from the heroes
of romance; in reality, the same 'ties' and the same 'bond' existed
in the world of Arthurian chivalry. Their 'ideological background'
cannot therefore provide an explanation of the transition from
epic to romance. Nor can the dates of St. Anselm and St. Bernard
help to explain what really happened. St. Anselm died in 1109,
St. Bernard in 1153, some twenty years before Chrétien wrote
his *Lancelot*. St. Bernard's lifetime coincides with the greatest
flowering of the *chansons de geste* and antedates by a few years the
appearance of the first example of romance. The 'spirit of the age'
which his teaching is supposed to embody may conceivably supply
a frame of reference for *both* kinds of narrative; but if it does, it
cannot in good logic have determined the change from one to the
other.

If, then, we are to look for the cause and the meaning of the
change in another direction it might be of interest, be it only by
way of a prelude, to begin by referring briefly to a text which
has no historical connection with the problem under discussion,

[1] Op. cit., p. 244.

but which can help us to transpose our thoughts into a different key. St. Augustine describes how another holy man, St. Ambrose, used to read.[1] He read, Augustine tells us, *to himself*, that is to say silently: 'his eyes wandered along the page and his heart searched out the sense, but his voice and tongue were at rest.'[2] This to St. Augustine seemed remarkable: he had never seen anyone read like that, and he thought that perhaps St. Ambrose wanted to avoid being questioned 'by some doubtful and attentive listener' or, more probably, wished to preserve his voice which was easily weakened. 'Whatever was his motive in so doing, doubtless in such a man it was a good one.' What St. Augustine could not have known was that in watching St. Ambrose read he was seeing the birth of a new world: that of the 'solitary reader who is accustomed to pass hours in the company of silent mental images evoked by written characters'.[3] The rise of romance in the twelfth century was something strangely similar: it was the birth of a world in which vernacular writings were to share with Latin texts the privilege of addressing the reader through the medium of visible, not audible symbols; through words intended to be read, not sung or even recited; and with this went a radical alteration of the very nature of literary experience. The change heralded our modern world in much the same way as St. Ambrose's silent approach to his text heralded our reading habits. In neither case did the new immediately supersede the old.[4]

In all the numerous writings about Old French epic two remarks made in passing and left undeveloped by their authors point the way to the answer we are seeking: one by W. P. Ker, the other by Gaston Paris. In describing the *Song of Roland* W. P. Ker says that

---

[1] *Confessiones*, VI. iii (*Patrologiae cursus completus*, xxxii. 720–1). Cf. J. Balogh, 'Voces paginarum', *Philologus* (1927), 83, 202; F. di Capua, 'Osservazioni sulla lettura e sulla preghiera ad alta voce presso i antichi', *Rendiconti della Accademia . . . di Napoli*, nuov. ser. 28 (1953) (Napoli, 1954), 59–62; and Dom Jean Leclercq, *L'Amour des lettres et le désir de Dieu* (Paris, 1957), 72. Dom Jean Leclercq describes the medieval reading habit as follows: 'Au moyen âge, on lit généralement en prononçant avec les lèvres, au moins à voix basse, par conséquent en entendant les phrases que les yeux voient.'

[2] 'Cum legebat, oculi ducebantur per paginas et cor intellectum rimabatur, vox autem et lingua quiescebant.'

[3] C. S. Lewis, *Allegory of Love* (Oxford, 1936), 65.

[4] Cf. Leclercq, op. cit., p. 25, n. 1.

it consists of 'separate scenes with no gradation or transition between them',[1] and Gaston Paris in his manual of Old French literature remarks that the poem strikes him as 'une suite d'explosions successives, toujours arrêtées court et toujours reprenant avec soudaineté'.[2] Both critics seem to have sensed in the poem the presence of loosely inter-related gestures and scenes, artistically valid as individual moments of great dramatic intensity, and yet dispensing with temporal and rational links and transitions. There is a parallel to this in the visual arts of the same period. Some of the great examples of eleventh- and twelfth-century pictorial narrative in Western Europe show the same concentration on 'separate scenes with no transition between them'. Professor Otto Pächt has drawn attention to the fact that in the Bayeux tapestry the gestures 'are never the organic result of the action in which the figures are involved. . . . It is the beholder who is addressed by these gestures; the actors of the drama speak to us, the spectators, not to the protagonists in whose company they appear on the stage.'[3] It is only in the beholder's mind, not in the painting, that the characters are linked with one another. In the same way, in the Durham 'Life' of St. Cuthbert depicting the life and miracles of the Northumbrian saint, the thread of the story is often 'lost in the process of creating a self-contained unit. One might say that each framed miniature makes a "picture", but not always a "story".'[4] The narrative function of such a picture can best be described as that of a a scene 'cut out from the flow of events'.[5] Of course, the analogy is not complete: the 'flow of events' is never entirely excluded from the *Song of Roland* or, for that matter, from any known epic poem; what is excluded is the consistent subordination of each single occurrence to a coherently developed scheme. The *Song of Roland* compels us to accept as a legitimate medium of poetic expression a language which dispenses with all the subtle means of co-ordination which we normally regard as a feature of literary style. The broad sweep of the richly nuanced sentence movement and the carefully structured dramatic dialogue,

---

[1] *Epic and Romance*, p. 290.
[2] *La Littérature française au moyen âge*, 5ème éd. (Paris, 1914), 62–3.
[3] *The Rise of Pictorial Narrative in Twelfth-Century England* (Oxford, 1962), 10.
[4] Ibid., p. 21. [5] Ibid., p. 31.

so characteristic of classical epic, are virtually absent from the epic of medieval France.[1] The assonant strophic pattern in the *Roland* gives every line the appearance of an independent unit; each strophe, or *laisse*, is in the words of Erich Auerbach 'like a bundle of sticks or spears of equal length, with similar points',[2] gathered together, pressed against each other, but never dissolved in a spacious easy-flowing syntactical movement. It is 'a paratactic structure consisting of very simple, extremely restricted, and yet often contradictory statements'.[3] There is even more to it than that. Parataxis normally means a loose arrangement of sentences; in the classical languages paratactic constructions belong to the low style: they are oral rather than written, comic and realistic rather than elevated.[4] They dispense with the entire apparatus of subordination and sequence and replace syntactic composition by mere juxtaposition of independent verbal units. But within this general definition there is room for two distinct forms of expression. The absence of causal connectives may be merely apparent; they may be there even though they are not expressed; our mind then rushes into the artificially created verbal vacuum to supply by its own cogitations all that the poet has deliberately left unsaid. In such cases parataxis is a mere device, productive of comic or sublime effects as the case may be—sometimes, as in the great examples of biblical narrative, creating a sense of depth and expectancy, the feeling that the unfathomable is there for us to discover, or at least to apprehend. The parataxis used in the French epic is of a different kind: it is genuine, not contrived; it invites simple acceptance, not elaboration; it does not conceal continuity and cohesion in silent intervals, but dispenses with such things, and any exegesis that attempts to supply them results in a distortion of the linguistic and poetic pattern of the work.

---

[1] Cf. Erich Auerbach, *Mimesis* (Bern, 1946), 108: 'Ausführliches, verbindendes Raisonnement, wie es die homerischen Helden lieben, kennen sie nicht, und ebensowenig gibt es bei ihnen frei ausströmende, treibende und drängende Ausdrucksbewegungen.'

[2] Ibid., p. 107: '. . . gleich als wären Stäbe oder Speere von gleicher Länge und mit ähnlich geformter Spitze zusammengebündelt'.

[3] Ibid., p. 103: '. . . ein parataktisches Gebilde von einfachen dabei doch oft sich widerspruchvollen äusserst engräumigen Satzungen'.

[4] Cf. Auerbach, op. cit., p. 110.

This feature of style has its counterpart in the most striking peculiarity of the genre, namely its use of 'repetition with variation', to which there is no exact parallel in our modern method of exposition. An event, or a scene, or a speech which forms the subject of a strophe may appear again in the next strophe with certain differences, not only of expression, but of substance; and it may be repeated again and again with variations; not simply with additional details, but with developments which represent departures from earlier statements. The aesthetic purpose of this device, known as 'le procédé des laisses similaires', was admirably described by Mildred K. Pope in a study which, although published half a century ago, has lost nothing of its interest and relevance.[1] She writes:

Whatever the origin of these *laisses* may be, their function in the *Chanson de Roland* is aesthetic. By describing the successive moments of crisis, by elaborating symmetrically the plaints over the dead, the poet has found an unequalled means of heightening the crisis, of emphasizing the emotional significance of the scene. In Ganelon's threefold praise of Charlemagne, the emir's threefold summons to his men, Oliver's threefold summons to Roland, Roland's threefold farewell to his sword, Charlemagne's fivefold lamentation over Roland, the poet's purpose and success are equally patent. . . . In passages like these the traditional strophe form offers him the chance of securing, by simplest means, most poignant, heart-stirring effects—and that chance he has taken.[2]

In a later portion of the same study a distinction is made between two types of *laisses similaires*: 'In the one we have set before us a repeated action, the representation of two, three or more separate but similar acts, described each in separate but similar *laisses*: in the other the poet gives us the detailed description of one single action or emotion: . . . the act gradually revealed in its entirety, the emotion under its different aspects.'[3] Examples of the latter

[1] 'Four *Chansons de Geste*: a Study in Old French Versification', *Modern Language Review*, viii (1913), 352 ff., ix (1914), 52 ff., x (1915), 310 ff.   [2] *M.L.R.* viii. 359.
[3] Ibid. x. 314. Among the recent studies attention should be drawn to Cesare Segre's 'Il "Boeci", i poemati agiografici e le origini delle forma epica' in *Atti dell'Accademia Nazionale dei Lincei*, vol. xv, pp. 270–85, which contains references to most of the important studies of the *laisses similaires* published since the early years of this century. Pp. 270–3 are of particular relevance to the above discussion.

type are found not only in all the numerous *regrets*, but in such passages as the death of Vivien and Guillaume's sorrow in the *Chanson de Guillelme*, or Ganelon's praise of Charlemagne, or the latter's sorrow for Roland in the *Chanson de Roland*. The two types, we are told, find their counterpart in the ballad, but while the first type 'meets us in ballad poetry at every turn', the second is comparatively rare because 'the ballad poet rarely spends his strength in description of any kind, least of all of an emotion'.[1] What critics do not seem to have noticed hitherto, however, is that in one important respect the ballad technique differs from *both* types of *laisses similaires*. In ballad poetry the variations in 'similar' stanzas, whether these belong to the first or the second type, generally form a coherent sequence; they either become complementary to one another or represent successive steps in the progress of the narrative. To take one of the best-known examples of this type of composition, in *Mother and Maiden* the first line—'He came all so still'—occurs in three successive stanzas, but the second line is repeated with significant variations: 'Where his mother was', 'To his mother's bower', 'Where his mother lay', forming a clear progression, or what historians of ballad poetry call 'incremental repetition': a development consisting of easily perceptible logical steps towards a climax.[2] The *laisses similaires* in the *Roland* and the *Chanson de Guillelme* are based on a much more complex pattern. A significant case is the description of Roland's death, which stretches over three successive *laisses*,

[1] *The Bonny Earl of Murray* is a somewhat unusual example of a ballad with a series of stanzas each of which describes the same situation 'under a slightly different aspect' (no. 181A in F. J. Child's ed. of *The English and Scottish Ballads*, 8 vols., 1857–9 and 1882–98), e.g. 'And the bonny Earl of Murray, Oh! he might have been a king!'; 'And the bonny Earl of Murray, Oh! he was the Queen's love!' Quoted by M. K. Pope, op. cit., x. 315.

[2] For other examples cf. *Sir Patrick Spens, Willies Lady, St. Stephen and Herod*, etc. Cf. also F. B. Gummere, *The Beginnings of Poetry*, p. 194 *et passim, The Popular Ballad*, p. 96 *et passim*; and W. M. Hart, *Ballad and Epic (Harvard Studies and Notes in Philology and Literature*, xi), pp. 227–87. Gummere writes (p. 91): 'Literal repetition yielded, for the sake of progress, to this repetition with increments, developing the situation; and incremental repetition came soon to be the close pattern of ballad stuff. Refrains may stay or vanish; in the record they cease to appeal to voice and ear and seem a waste of energy; but incremental repetition can wane only by the slow process of "making over", by excision and correction, from one version to another. Hence its great significance. It supplies a visible link between oldest choral repetition and actual text.'

each referring to the same scene; and yet the result in each case is neither a simple expansion of the preceding *laisse* nor a new phase of the narrative. First Roland 'à faibles coups et souvent, bat sa coulpe. / Pour ses péchés il tend vers Dieu son gant'.[1] Then 'de l'une de ses mains il frappe sa poitrine: Dieu, par ta grâce, mea culpa, pour mes péchés, les grands et les menus, que j'ai faits depuis l'heure où je naquis jusqu'à ce jour où je me vois abattu. Il a tendu vers Dieu son gant droit. Les anges du ciel descendent à lui.'[2] Finally, in the third *laisse*, 'il bat sa coulpe et demande à Dieu merci: Vrai Père qui jamais ne mentis, toi qui rappelas saint Lazare d'entre les morts, toi qui sauvas Daniel des lions, sauve mon âme de tous périls, pour les péchés que j'ai faits dans ma vie! Il a offert à Dieu son gant droit: saint Gabriel l'a pris dans sa main.'[3] These are not three different moments of time, but three independent descriptions of the same moment; and yet the details of each description are not intended, as in a ballad, to coalesce into a single picture. Each description is a separate vision of the same event, so presented that the scene would lose much of its significance if all the passages referring to it were telescoped into one.[4]

We look nowadays upon a narrative of events as a *temporal* sequence, each element of which moves towards the next as each

---

[1] ll. 2364–5. The translation is Bédier's. It follows the original word for word as no existing English translation does in this instance.

[2] ll. 2368–74:

> A l'une main si ad sun piz batud:
> 'Deus, meie culpe vers les tues vertuz
> De mes pecchez, des granz e des menuz,
> Que jo ai fait dés l'ure que nez fui
> Tresqu'a cest jur que ci sui consoüt.'
> Sun destre guant en ad vers Deu tendut.
> Angles del ciel i descendent a lui.

[3] ll. 2383–90:

> Cleimet sa culpe, si priet Deu mercit:
> 'Veire Patene, ki unkez ne mentis,
> Seint Lazaron de mort resurrexis
> E Daniel des leons guaresis,
> Guaris de mei l'anme de tuz perilz
> Pur les pecchez que en ma vie fis!'
> Sun destre guant a Deu en puroffrit.
> Seint Gabriel de sa main l'ad pris.

[4] For a more detailed analysis of this passage see my article on 'La Mort de Roland' in the *Cahiers de civilisation médiévale*, Apr.–June 1964, pp. 138–41, reproduced in full in *A la recherche d'une poétique médiévale*, pp. 49–74.

moment of time moves towards the one that follows; and at the
same time we see it as a *rational* sequence so arranged that each
phase of it is related in a definable manner to whatever comes before
or after. What is so difficult for us to understand is that a great
masterpiece such as the *Song of Roland* should triumphantly discard
the twin principles of rational and temporal motivation. When
Roland is appointed, on Ganelon's advice, commander of the
rearguard of the French army, Roland's reaction to this is expressed
in two consecutive, but seemingly contradictory stanzas. First he
replies,[1] addressing Ganelon as his *parastre*: 'I must hold you very
dear: you have adjudged the rearguard to me. Charles, the king
who holds France, shall lose thereby neither palfrey nor charger,
neither mule nor hinny, neither hack nor sumpter which has not
first been fought for with a sword.' And Ganelon says: 'You speak
true, I know it well.' The next laisse is equally brief:[2] 'When
Roland hears that he will be in the rearguard he speaks angrily
to his stepfather: "You wretch, bad man of ignoble birth, did
you think the glove would drop from my hand as the staff did
for you before Charles?" '—a reminder of what happened when
earlier on in the poem Ganelon, on Roland's suggestion, was
appointed to what seemed an equally dangerous mission. This
is followed by a third *laisse*[3] addressed this time to the emperor himself and expressing Roland's devotion to him and his determination
to serve him. At the emotional level there is no difficulty about
this curious sequence: Roland's expression of gratitude to Ganelon
stems from his unconquerable, ferocious pride, characteristically
conveyed by the enumeration of the various mounts and beasts
of burden, not one of which will be surrendered without a fight.
But pride and defiance can equally well take the form of hatred
and contempt; hence Roland's second speech, every word of which
asserts his scornful triumph over the man he despises. The first
time he speaks as befits a knight—*a lei de chevalier*—the second
time scornfully, angrily, *ireement*, and there is no articulate transition, no suggestion even of a link between the two speeches.
Gaston Paris, and many critics after him, thought that there was
no room for two such contradictory statements in the poem:

[1] ll. 753-60.   [2] ll. 761-5.   [3] ll. 766-73.

'le même poète n'a pu prêter à son héros deux sentiments aussi contradictoires sur le même sujet'.[1] The formula is admirable in its precision and aptness; it raises the whole issue to the level of a fundamental aesthetic problem. Is it possible for the same poet to make his hero express contradictory views on the same subject? If it is not, then one of the two strophes must be deleted from the text, and several editors have in fact removed one of them, in most cases the second. Bédier has tried to save them both by showing that the contradiction was more apparent than real.[2] But even he did not deny the principle formulated by Gaston Paris; even he did not feel he could go as far as to say that a poet could give his hero 'deux sentiments contradictoires sur le même sujet'.[3]

The difficulty increases as we progress from the consideration of individual passages to a view of the poem as a whole. As we follow the progress of the battle of Roncevaux we are tempted, against our better judgement, to forget that we are dealing with a type of poetry which is concerned exclusively with action and statement, not with motives; we are tempted to ask why Roland was chosen for the part he was to play in the disaster, why, when attacked by a superior force of Saracens, he decided to let his men die fighting against insuperable odds rather than ask Charlemagne for help. To these questions there is no adequate answer. The conflict between the reckless courage of Roland and the sound strategy of Oliver is there, but it is not there to be discussed or explained. When it is the poet's turn to speak, he is content to say that Roland is brave and Oliver is wise. Neither on this nor on any other occasion does he attempt to comment on the meaning of the action, and it is an unwarranted simplification to suggest, as critics usually do, that no comment is called for because the motives behind the action are crystal-clear. They are far from clear; and if they are not explained it is not because the poet wishes to leave them to our imagination, nor because he prefers suggestion to analysis, but because he is more interested in the progress of events than in coherent motivation. Not that the *Chanson de*

---

[1] *Histoire poétique de Charlemagne* (Paris, 1865), 22.
[2] *La Chanson de Roland commentée* par Joseph Bédier, pp. 151-2.
[3] Cf. *Cahiers de civilisation médiévale*, loc. cit.

Roland has no 'thematic' implications, no 'meaning' apart from its narrative content. It is a theme in movement, but at no point is the movement arrested or suspended in order to make time for a reflection on the theme—for what Northrop Frye calls 'the *mythos* in stasis'.[1] Nor is there any reason why time should be made for such things. Why indeed should it be part of the poet's—*any* poet's —task to elucidate his narrative in terms of a chain of cause and effect? E. M. Forster asks this very question. While admitting that a rationally devised plot 'is exciting and may be beautiful', he wonders whether it is not a fetish borrowed from the drama, 'from the spatial limitations of the stage'. 'Cannot fiction devise a framework that is not so logical, yet more suitable to its genius?'[2]

The *Chanson de Roland*, like some other French epic poems, may serve as an example of such a framework. The climax of the battle of Roncevaux, Roland's death, is not the outcome of a series of rationally motivated events. Roland is not even killed in battle: he dies because as he sounds the horn *a dulor e a paine* his temples burst, and no one can say that by normal standards of motivation an accident of this kind can justify the death of a hero in whom is vested the glory of his race. What is even more remarkable is that any explanation that we might contribute ourselves would inevitably detract from our aesthetic appreciation, and consequently from our understanding, of the poem. Karl Vossler observes that the essence of the French epic as represented by the *Song of Roland* is 'affective and impressionistic' and that the Roland poet works 'with affective values and contrasts between affective values'.[3] When in *Hérodias* Flaubert makes nine verses in the Gospel according to St. Matthew into a *conte*, he traces the sequence of events that lead up to the execution of John the Baptist, and the story he offers us is a convincing interpretation, marked by deep psychological insight, of the motives that impel the principal characters to act as they do. The sequence is not only

    [1] *Anatomy of Criticism* (Princeton, 1957), 53 *et passim*.
    [2] *Aspects of the Novel* (London, 1927), 93.
    [3] *Langue et culture de la France*, préface et traduction d'Alphonse Juilland (Paris (Payot), 1953), 48: 'Au lieu d'adopter une perspective sensorielle, l'auteur travaille en vrai rhétoriqueur, en utilisant les valeurs de sentiment et leurs contrastes . . . Les événements sont présentés et ordonnés suivant leur valeur sentimentale et non pas d'après leur connexion logique et leur déroulement chronologique.'

orderly, but ordered, and causally ordered; motivation proceeds
by logical steps from known causes to unknown but inevitable
effects, or from known effects to their hidden but detectable causes.
It would be a mistake to think that this is a pattern *unknown* to the
Roland poet; all we can infer is that the Roland poet does not
seem to think he has to adhere to it *consistently*. When Roland
nominates Ganelon as Charlemagne's ambassador to the Saracen
king, Ganelon flies into a towering passion and accuses Roland of
plotting his death; and he is convinced that by plotting in his
turn the ambush at Roncevaux he will only be meeting treachery
with treachery. But if this were the real motivation of his behaviour
and of the subsequent defeat of the rearguard of Charlemagne's
army, it would be a singularly inadequate one. By all reasonable
standards Ganelon's mission to Saragossa involves no serious
risk for him. Marsile has been defeated by Charlemagne. The only
way in which he can avoid disaster is by persuading Charlemagne,
through Ganelon, to grant him favourable terms of peace. Ganelon
is the bearer of a generous offer, and there is no reason at all why
Marsile should commit an act of violence against him. Allusions
to the fate of Basan and Basile, two unfortunate messengers sent
by Charlemagne to Marsile and beheaded out of hand,[1] have no
bearing on the case. All that such allusions suggest is the necessity
to accept their irrelevance, however difficult this may be.[2]

What is relevant is the way in which the poet maintains the
emotional tone of the narrative, the fact that the final catastrophe
emerges not out of an articulated causal scheme, but, with height-
ened intensity, out of a series of logically unconnected but emo-
tionally significant events and situations. There is no need for
the poet to *explain*; as Auerbach has it, 'the things which happen
are stated with paratactic bluntness: everything must happen as
it does happen, it could not be otherwise.'[3] The life of the infidel
knights seems hardly different from that of the Christians: both
sides believe in their deeds of prowess as a road to Heaven, both

[1] *La Chanson de Roland*, ll. 207–9, 488–91.
[2] This interpretation of the Ganelon episode was suggested to me by the late Dr.
Whitehead, the most reliable modern editor of the poem. It was part of his commentary on the text which has remained unpublished to this day.
[3] Op. cit., p. 102. Eng. tr. by W. R. Trask (Princeton, 1953), 101.

are graced with the status of knighthood, and in both cases knighthood—*vasselage*—is understood as readiness to die fighting the enemies of one's faith. Why, then, should we believe the poet when he says: *paien unt tort et chrestiens unt dreit*?[1] And why, to sum up all such doubts in a single question, why should Roland die a martyr's death at Roncevaux?

When these and other similar questions arise in our minds and we hasten to supply the answers, we do so because we are convinced that it is what the poet intended us to do. A closer view of early French epic poetry would show that the poet's mode of exposition required no such effort on the reader's or the listener's part. It was calculated to produce a reaction of a vastly different kind. It was a mode which sought not to enlighten, but to move and to impress—not a questioning or an explanatory, but a lyrical and a descriptive mode. An exegesis that would reduce the matter of such poetry to questions and answers would distort its very essence; it would be grossly misleading in that it would deal with non-existent issues and ignore the real ones; for it is not until the questioning mode has conquered man's imagination that an exegesis of this kind can be considered at all relevant. To see this happen we must wait about half-a-century—long enough to witness the final triumph of romance.

[1] l. 1015.

II

THE DISCOVERY OF MEANING

THE difficulty of defining romance lies mainly in the fact that its most important distinguishing feature is inseparable from what we normally understand by 'literature'. We take it for granted that a reader should use his reasoning faculty, meditate in silence upon the meaning of the facts presented to him, and cultivate the 'thematic' mode as opposed to the purely 'fictional': a mode which is above all a questioning one.[1] What we fail to realize is that in terms of Western literary history these things are of comparatively recent date. They have been known in more remote areas, as they were known in the Greek and Roman world; but medieval Europe had to discover them afresh, and it is by no means immaterial to know how and when the rediscovery occurred.[2]

In his famous eulogy of his great contemporary, Hartmann von Aue, Gottfried von Strassburg writes: 'Look how Hartmann von Aue embellishes his tale with words and thoughts [*mit worten und mit sînnen*] . . . and how he transfixes the meaning [*meine*] of the events he narrates.'[3] *Meine* stands here for the 'significance', perhaps even the 'message', of the story; *sîn*, on the other hand, might mean not

---

[1] Cf. Northrop Frye, *Anatomy of Criticism*, loc. cit., for illustrations of the various possible degrees of fictional and thematic interest. Professor Frye points out that although *Tom Jones* is named after its plot and *Sense and Sensibility* after its theme, 'Fielding has as strong a thematic interest as Jane Austen has in telling a good story. Both novels are strongly fictional in emphasis compared to *Uncle Tom's Cabin* or *The Grapes of Wrath*.'

[2] The now fashionable insistence on the importance of classical learning as the common denominator of all forms of medieval poetry has obscured this feature of romance. Cf. Edmond Faral, *Recherches sur les sources latines des contes et romans courtois du moyen âge* (Paris, 1913), 24, n. 1, 25–6, and F. M. Warren, 'Some Features of Style in Early French Narrative Poetry', *Modern Philology*, iii (1905), 179 ff., 513 ff.

[3] 'Hartman der Ouwære, / ahî, wie der diu mære / beid' ûzen unde innen / mit worten und mit sînnen / durchvärwet und durchzieret! / wie er mit rede figieret / der âventiure meine!' Gottfried von Strassburg, *Tristan*, herausgegeben von Reinhold Bechstein (4th ed.), i. 168, ll. 4619–25.

only 'thought' but 'sense'[1] and 'wisdom';[2] elsewhere in Gottfried it means 'scheming', 'cunning', and even 'deceit'.[3] It could connote any kind of deliberate intervention on the author's part intended to give the work the sort of direction, slant, or significance that he thought appropriate.

There is evidence to show that half a century before Gottfried the concepts represented by these terms were familiar to French writers. In the Prologue to her *Lais* Marie de France describes in the following words what she thinks a romance writer's task should be:

It was the custom of the ancients, [she writes] as witnessed by Priscian, to speak obscurely in the books they wrote so that those who came later and studied those books might construe the text (*gloser la lettre*) and add their own thoughts (*de lor sen le surplus mettre*).[4]

Any work of adaptation—which, in medieval terms, is to all intents and purposes synonymous with what we would call a work of literature—must, then, according to Marie de France, depend for its success on a judicious use of two devices: the discovery of the meaning implicit in the matter, and the insertion of such thoughts (*sen*) as might adorn, or be read into, the matter. The French word *sen* stems from the Germanic *sîn*, but its use in Old French was affected by its near homonym derived from the Latin *sensu(m)*, and its semantic spectrum ranged as a result very widely, extending to such concepts as 'purpose'[5] at one end of the scale and 'skill'[6] at the other, and covering a variety of intervening meanings: 'thought',[7] 'wisdom', 'understanding', etc.[8] 'To add

---

[1] As at ll. 4689 ff. where 'thought' and 'sense' are equally acceptable renderings.

[2] As at ll. 11468–9: 'daz ist sîn'.

[3] As at l. 2299: 'mit deheiner slahte sînnen'. I am greatly indebted to Professor F. P. Pickering for his enlightening comments on all these passages in Gottfried.

[4] 'Costume fus as anciëns, / Ce testimoine Preciëns, / Es livres que jadis faisoient / Assez oscurement disoient / Por ceus qui a venir estoient / Et qui aprendre les devoient, / Qu'il peüssent gloser la lettre / Et de lor sen le surplus mettre' (ed. Hoepffner, ll. 9–16).

[5] *Rom. de Troie*, ll. 18378–80 (*en tel sen*).

[6] *Erec et Enide*, ll. 6743–5 (*de toz sanz*).

[7] Often combined with *painne* (=effort).

[8] *Rom. de Troie*, ll. 549–50. At ll. 121–2 the phrase *sen et engin* is used in the sense of 'skill and craft'.

one's own *sen* could, therefore, be taken to mean to 'enliven' the matter, not only with one's thoughts, but with one's understanding, purpose, and skill. What a good romance writer is expected to do, then, according to both Gottfried von Strassburg and Marie de France, is to reveal the *meaning* of the story (its *meine*), adding to it such embellishing thoughts as he considers appropriate; by doing this he would raise his work to a level of distinction which no straightforward narration could ever reach.

For students of medieval exegesis such pronouncements have a familiar ring. Hervé de Bourgdieu, probably the best exponent of monastic exegesis in the first half of the twelfth century, justifies his belief in the virtues of interpretation by saying that it surpasses the narrative as fruit surpasses the leaves of the tree upon which it grows.[1] 'The story is chaff', says the author of the *Livre des Rois*, 'the meaning wheat; the meaning is the fruit, the story the branch.'[2] And when Drogo of Paris praises the work of his friend Berengar of Tours, it is clear that he looks upon a skilful interpretation of a sacred text as the highest form of learning.[3] Hence the pride felt by twelfth-century romance writers in the possession of a similar skill in the secular sphere, and their delight in the practice of a craft unknown to earlier writers in the vernacular. The craft is indeed so new that it is still visible: no part of it is concealed; it stands exposed, like the mechanism of a clock in a glass case, for everyone to watch and to admire.[4]

This craft, however, like the art of biblical exposition, was the product not so much of learning as of certain habits of mind acquired *through* learning. Much emphasis has recently been placed, especially in the medieval English field, on the so-called 'patristic

[1] '... quantum poma foliis, tantum allegoria historiis praecellit' (cf. Stegmüller, *Repertorium biblicum medii aevi*, iii, no. 3256).
[2] 'L'estorie est paille, le sen est grains; le sen est fruit, l'estorie raims' (ed. Curtius, p. 5).
[3] Cf. A. J. Macdonald, *Berengar and the Reform of Sacramental Doctrine* (London, 1930), 32.
[4] W. P. Ker (op. cit., p. 324) rightly remarks that it is useless to go to those French books in order to catch the first jet of romantic fancy, the 'silly sooth' of the golden age; for the romance writers were 'as fully conscious of their craft as any later poet who borrowed from them their giants and enchanters, their forests and their magic castles'.

exegesis'. The romance writers were no doubt aware of the techniques of exegesis, witness Chaucer's mention of Peter Riga's
Aurora and the freedom with which Langland, Chaucer, and others
—among them many French writers—'employed references to
glossing and the general apparatus of biblical commentary, often
as the vehicle of metaphor'.[1] But they also knew that, according to
Thomas Aquinas, 'in no intellectual activity of the human mind
(*in nulla scientia humana industria inventa*) can there, properly speaking,
be found anything but literal sense: only in Scripture, of which the
Holy Ghost was the author and man the instrument, can there be
found the *sensus spiritualis*.'[2] St. Augustine himself, in spite of his
famous plea for taking 'further meanings' in the thing signified by
the word,[3] had warned the commentators of the sacred texts that
they must not 'understand figuratively passages which ought to be
understood literally'.[4] What can hardly be denied, however, is
the common intellectual origin of the interpretative nature of
romance on the one hand and of the exegetic tradition on the other.
Both reflect the teaching provided by the great cathedral schools
of France in the twelfth century.[5] It was there that future romance
writers as well as prospective expositors of the Bible received the
essential part of their training. By far the most significant aspect
of that training was the emphasis on Grammar.[6] Writing in the
last quarter of the twelfth century, Gautier de Châtillon says that
'among the *artes* which are called the *trivium* Grammar takes
precedence as the first foundation. Under her serve the troop of

[1] R. E. Kaske in *Critical Approaches to Medieval Literature*, ed. Dorothy Bethurum
(New York, 1960), 30.
[2] *Quaestiones Quodlibetales*, VII, Quaestio vi, Art. xvi. Quoted by E. Talbot Donald-
son in *Critical Approaches to Medieval Literature*, pp. 4, 135. Cf. *Sum. Theol.* I. i. 9–10.
[3] *De Doctrina*, III. v (9); *Patrologia Latina*, xxxiv. 69.
[4] *De Doctrina*, III, x (14); *Patrologia Latina*, xxxiv. 71.
[5] Cf. *Histoire de la littérature française illustrée*, publiée sous la direction de Joseph
Bédier et Paul Hazard, p. 16: 'C'est dans ces écoles que les auteurs de nos romans
courtois ont fait leur apprentissage, et ils trouvèrent dans les cours royales et
seigneuriales où la culture avait plus ou moins profondément pénétré, un large
accueil. . . . Les charges et offices de l'Église ne suffisaient plus à absorber tous les
clercs à leur sortie des écoles épiscopales ou abbatiales. Il y eut, semble-t-il, pléthore
et crise. Beaucoup de ces clercs inemployés cherchèrent dans le monde laïque des
moyens de tirer parti de leur savoir.'
[6] Cf. M. D. Chenu, 'Grammaire et théologie aux XIIᵉ et XIIIᵉ siècles', *Archives
d'histoire doctrinale et littéraire du moyen âge*, 1936, pp. 5–28.

those who write in verse';[1] and one of his contemporaries, Étienne de Tournai, in describing the education of a boy, visualizes poetry approaching the pupil 'at the instigation of Grammar':

Venit ad Grammatice Poesis hortatum.[2]

The term itself had since classical times undergone a considerable extension of meaning. For Plato and Aristotle the 'art of grammar' was concerned simply with the correct use of Greek; but under the influence of Alexandrian writers, and especially of Dionysius Thrax, the phrase came to mean, in addition, the art of interpreting works of poetry.[3] Through Varro this dual conception of the grammatical discipline established itself in the Roman tradition.[4] For Quintilian Grammar was, on the one hand, the science of correct expression ('scientia recte loquendi'), and on the other, the art of interpreting the works of the poets ('poetarum enarratio').[5] Other Roman writers extended the 'exegetic' function of Grammar to works of narrative prose.[6] At the time of the great revival of classical learning in twelfth-century France the schools of Chartres, Orleans, and Paris seem to have conceived and practised the teaching of Grammar in precisely this fashion: as a

---

[1] Cf. *Moralisch-satirische Gedichte Walters von Châtillon*, ed. K. Strecker (1929), no. 41, v. 7.

[2] Ernst Robert Curtius (op. cit., p. 53) quotes this line, but confines his comment to the remark that 'poetry was assigned sometimes to grammar, sometimes to rhetoric'. In an article in the *Zeitschrift für romanische Philologie* (lviii. 479) he asks: 'Welche Folgen für das literarische Schaffen ergaben sich aus der Bindung der Poesie an Grammatik und Rhetorik?' His *European Literature and the Latin Middle Ages* is to a large extent an answer to this question couched in 'topological' terms. No real attempt has so far been made to answer it in terms of narrative technique.

[3] Cf. Karl Barwick, 'Remmius Palaemon und die römische Ars Grammatika', *Philologus*, Supplement, Band XV (Leipzig, 1922), 216: 'Diese alexandrinische Auffassung der Grammatik, die man als Kritik und Exegese der Autoren bezeichnen darf, ist (wenn auch mannigfach modifiziert) dem ganzen Altertum nich abhanden gekommen. Gelegentlich wird sie, als die jüngere, der älteren gegenübergestellt, und die eine als große und vollkommenere, die andere als kleine oder unvollkommene Grammatik bezeichnet.'

[4] Cf. ibid., pp. 225–6, 230–2. See also Hellfried Dahlmann, *Varro und die hellenistische Sprachtheorie* (Berlin, 1932), 44 ff.

[5] *Institutio Oratoria*, ed. Colson, I. iv. 2. Cf. Isidore, *Etym.* I. 41. 2.

[6] *Scientia poetas et historicos intellegere* (Marii Victorini *Ars grammatica*, ed. H. Keil, p. 4). Diomedes, Dositheus, and Donatus give virtually the same definition, with varying degrees of emphasis on the exegetic aspect of the discipline. Cf. K. Barwick, op. cit., pp. 220–3 and H. Marrou, *Histoire de l'éducation dans l'antiquité* (Paris, 1948), 372.

means of acquiring not only linguistic knowledge but the ability to elucidate and to comment upon certain chosen examples of Latin verse and prose. Alexander Neckam, in his *De laudibus divinae sapientiae*, compares Orleans to Parnassus and says that 'in no other city were the songs of the Muses watched over with so much zeal or better interpreted'.[1] And for John of Salisbury Grammar as taught at Chartres was 'the sweet companion of hidden thoughts',[2] a *primary* art without which a man would proceed in vain to the rest. It was, to be sure, an artifice, a device to be learnt by dint of exercises, not unlike the *lecture expliquée* of our own day, its modern counterpart and its direct descendant; but like any such artifice it was capable of acting as a stimulus.[3] It certainly instilled in the pupil's mind the habit of bringing out the significance of whatever he found not fully explained in his *auctores*—a habit of mind which in a writer could easily become a habit of conception.[4] And so it

[1]
>Non se Parnassus tibi conferat, Aurelianis,
>Parnassi vertex cedet uterque tibi,
>Carmina Pieridum, multum vigilata labore,
>Exponi nulla certius urbe reor.

(*De laudibus*, ll. 607–10, quoted by L. V. Delisle, 'Les écoles d'Orléans au douzième siècle', *Bulletin de la Société de l'Histoire de France*, vii (1869), 146.) Cf. also John of Salisbury, *Metalogicon*, ed. C. C. J. Webb, 854 a–b, p. 54. Orleans and Chartres maintained their position long after in the University of Paris 'the green fields of authors' had withered, in John Garland's phrase, under the 'jealous blast' of dialectic, scholastic philosophy, and theology:

>Auctorum vernans exaruit area, pratum
>Florigerum boreas flatu livente percussit

(*Ars lectoria ecclesiae*, Bruges, MS. 456, f. 76ᵛ, printed in J. L. Paetow, *The Arts Course at Mediaeval Universities*, p. 16.)

[2] 'Dulcis secretorum comes.' Cf. op. cit., pp. 58–9.

[3] Cf. E. R. Curtius, *Europäische Literatur*, p. 393: 'Zwischen Kunst und Künstelei sind die Übergänge fliessend. Das genetische Verhältnis zwischen beiden ist keineswegs eindeutig. Man pflegt in der Künstelei ein Spätprodukt und eine Verfallserscheinung zu sehen: Entartung von Kunst. Aber auch das Umgekehrte kann eintreten. Die Stilgeschichte des lateinischen Mittelalters beweist es hundertfach. Spätantike Sprachkünstelei wurde ein technischer Ansporn und weckte artistischen Ehrgeiz.' Cf. also Dom Jean Leclercq, op. cit., pp. 125–6.

[4] It would, however, be misleading to suggest that the type of narrative represented by the early epics disappeared when the new type was introduced. The 'non-interpretative' narrative survives even today at all levels of simplicity and sophistication. It is, as C. S. Lewis once pointed out to me, still dominant among country people who, if asked any question about *their* narrative, usually repeat the *fact*. At the other end of the scale, the technique of bare statement, free from any consideration of cause and effect, is rapidly gaining ground in the finest examples of contemporary fiction.

came about that when a 'literate' writer set himself the task of making a traditional or a classical story into a romance, nothing seemed more important to him than the process of elucidating his material. The modern reader may well feel that some of the resulting additions were unnecessary and that in many cases the stories could safely have been left to speak for themselves; but every age and, indeed, every nation has its own standard of 'necessity', and the mere fact of expressing in an articulate manner what is already known may, under certain conditions, be conceived as an essential part of the writer's task. Nor is that type of elucidation bound by what the glossators of sacred texts called the 'literal' sense—*sententia litteralis scripturae ab auctore intenta*;[1] the meaning set forth by the explicator could be the equivalent of what Hugo of St. Victor described as the 'deeper insight'—*profundior intelligentia*—not to be found except by exposition and interpretation.[2]

The resulting commentary could be of two kinds—'interlinear' or 'marginal'—as may be seen from the example following this page (Plate II). As the practice developed, it became necessary in some cases to separate the commentary from the text altogether and make it into a self-contained volume. Peter Lombard's commentary on St. Paul was not only made into such a volume, but was promoted to the rank of a text in its own right, and caused the appearance of further *glossae*, this time by Pierre de Poitiers, again in the form of a separate book.[3] Nor was there any reason why the process could not have been carried further; but at this point Marie de France's formula—*gloser la lettre*—has to be supplemented by what she says in the next line: *de lor sen le sorplus mettre*. What she

[1] Cf. Friedrich Ohly, 'Vom geistigen Sinn des Wortes im Mittelalter', *Zeitschrift für deutsches Altertum und deutsche Literatur*, lxxxix (1958), 1–21, and especially his comments on Chrétien de Troyes and Gottfried von Strassburg on pp. 18–20.

[2] Cf. *Didascalicon*, ed. C. H. Bultimer (Washington, 1939), III. viii. 58. On the history of spiritual exposition see Beryl Smalley, *The Study of the Bible in the Middle Ages* (Oxford, 1941), 199–241, and C. Spieq, *Esquisse d'une histoire de l'exégèse latine au moyen âge* (Paris, 1944), *passim*. Owen Barfield (*Saving the Appearances*, p. 74) gives a useful warning against making too sharp a distinction between the 'literal' and the 'symbolical' in a medieval context. The two were in fact capable of being combined and the phenomena themselves could carry 'the sort of multiple significance which we today only find in symbols'. Cf. also Charles Donahue in *Critical Approaches to Medieval Literature*, ed. Dorothy Bethurum, p. 76; and *La Renaissance du XIIᵉ siècle: les écoles et l'enseignement*, par G. Paré, A. Brunet, P. Tremblay (Paris–Ottawa, 1933), 116–21.   [3] Cf. G. Paré *et al.*, op. cit., pp. 118–19.

has in mind there is an extended form of commentary which goes beyond the limits of 'grammatical interpretation' and involves the use of the author's own thoughts—the practice of his own imagination, in accordance with the principles embodied in Rhetoric: the first part of the Trivium imperceptibly shades into the second. In Roman times Rhetoric was conceived as a means of conveying the speaker's conception of the case, his way of looking at the events and the people concerned;[1] it was also, according to Martianus Capella, the means by which the orator could display his talent 'despite the meagreness of the case'.[2] What a speaker trained in the use of Rhetoric felt naturally compelled to do was not simply to elucidate the matter but to adapt it to a given point of view.[3] Carried one stage further this method was bound to result in the remodelling of the matter itself, or at least of those parts of it which were at variance with the thoughts and feelings one wished to convey.[4] Rhetoric could thus lead to a purposeful refashioning of traditional material, and the adaptor could become to all intents and purposes an original author, except that, unlike some authors, he would care above all for the *way* in which he told his stories[5] and measure his achievement in terms of such new significance as he was able to confer upon an existing body of facts.

[1] Gaston Boissier, 'Les Écoles de déclamation à Rome', *Revue des Deux Mondes* (1902), x 491.

[2] *De Nuptiis Philologiae et Mercurii*, ed. Dick, ll. 246–7.

[3] Cf. Theodore Haarhoff, *Schools of Gaul* (Oxford, 1920), 68: 'The grammarian used his knowledge to expand the text, the rhetor his imagination.' So far as the twelfth century is concerned we are less well informed about the teaching of rhetoric than about that of grammar, although much can be deduced from the surviving 'reading lists' used in the schools of Paris and Chartres. Cf. C. H. Haskins in *Havard Studies in Classical Philology*, xx (1900), 75–90 and A. Clerval, *Les Écoles de Chartres au moyen âge* (Paris, 1895), 222. Cf. also Ennodius, *Dictiones*, xxvii.

[4] Why did this have to wait till the twelfth century to take effect? One possible answer is suggested by the evidence of integration of *ethica* and *grammatica* just at that time. Cf. Philippe Delhaye, *Recherches de théologie ancienne et médiévale*, xxv (1958), 59–110, who writes as follows: 'Le professeur de grammaire ne se contente pas d'étudier les textes classiques pour y trouver l'application des règles ou les beautés littéraires. Il souligne *ex professo* les leçons de morale qui y sont inclues . . . Ce sont des clercs qui veulent justifier aux yeux de leur conscience l'étude des classiques.'

[5] Cf. Friedrich Ohly, op. cit., pp. 19–20: 'Daß mittelalterliche Dichter ohne Sorge um ihren Dichterruhm fremde Stoffe übernehmen konnten, wie neben vielen anderen Fallen die deutschen Dichter die französischen Romane, um an ihnen weiterzudeuten zu ihrer Sinnerhellung, haben wir im Zusammenhang damit zu sehen, daß es dem Mittelalter nicht so sehr auf Neufindung von Stoffen als auf deren neue Deutung ankommt (ein wesentlicher Unterschied zu dem, was die Moderne

II. A NINTH-CENTURY MANUSCRIPT OF VIRGIL'S FIFTH ECLOGUE with interlinear and marginal annotation

(MS. Bodl. Canon. Class. Lat. 50, f. 7)

Photograph Bodleian Library

These distinctions were new in twelfth-century vernacular literature, and Chrétien de Troyes was, so far as we know, the first French writer to formulate them. In the opening lines of his *Conte de la Charrette* he said that he owed both its *matiere* and its *sen*, meaning presumably 'significance' or 'purpose', to his patroness, Marie de Champagne: *matiere et san l'an donne e livre.* The marriage of matter and meaning, of narrative and commentary, was the key to the new kind of narrative poetry—the poetry that assumed in the reader both the ability and the desire to think of an event in terms of what one's mind could build upon it, or descry behind it. One is reminded of Master Léonin, *optimus organista*, an exact contemporary of Chrétien de Troyes and the real founder of the art of polyphony which was essentially an art of building musical commentaries—*organa dupla*, or two-part *organa*—upon traditional chants. The possibility of adding such commentaries was *implied* in every one of these chants, but never *realized* until the idea of a *sen* had crossed the mind of a great musician. What happened then was exactly parallel to what the poets did when they elaborated a traditional tale in a direction which might be thought to have been implied in it from the beginning.[1]

The initiators of this technique in the field of secular narrative were Chrétien's immediate predecessors, the authors of romances based upon classical subjects: *Thebes*, *Troie*, and *Enéas*—all written probably between 1150 and 1160. Lavinia, having seen Aeneas, tells us in fifty lines (8083–133) how greatly his mere appearance has impressed her, and then suddenly interrupts her speech by asking herself: '*Fole, qu'as tu dit?*' Fifteen lines follow in which her heart and her reason argue the case between them. She knows that she has to marry Turnus—what then will she do with her love for Aeneas? Is she to belong to both? At this point another

vom Dichter erwarten).' There is no better way of saying that from the medieval point of view the elucidation of a given matter is of no smaller poetic value than original invention. Ohly sees in Cervantes the last link in the chain of 'interpreters' of a theme invented by Chrétien and never quite exhausted until the hero had become Don Quixote.

[1] The scholastic *manifestatio* is another expression of the same attitude of mind. Erwin Panofsky's well-known essay on *Gothic Architecture and Scholasticism* (London, 1957) is an attempt to show the possible relation of *manifestatio* to certain architectural concepts. His findings would have been even more impressive had he realized that he was dealing with a much more general phenomenon.

'self' intervenes and speaks to her in the first person singular, thus completing the pattern of what was to become in later literature the so-called interior monologue. Aeneas proceeds likewise: he too is, as it were, divided against himself, and his *alter ego* addresses him without much ceremony, telling him to keep quiet and that his love is sheer folly. Earlier on in the poem Dido's complaint was expressed through a dialogue—a conversation with her sister and confidante Anna; and according to one critic this transference of the deliberative function from the dialogue to a monologue corresponds to a transition from the technique of story-telling to that of organized fiction: from being a narrator the author becomes a novelist.[1]

Not that the mere introduction of the interior monologue is sufficient to create this new form of art. In the Old French version of the story of the Trojan War, *Le Roman de Troie* by Benoît de Sainte-Maure, a poem based upon Dares's *De Excidio* and Dictys's *Ephemeris Belli Trojani*, Achilles, in contrast to his silent classical prototype, bursts into a long soliloquy describing the devastating effects of his love for Polyxena,[2] a theme suggested by Dares.[3] Achilles' complaint contributes little to the progress of the action, still less to our knowledge of the human heart, but Benoît de Sainte-Maure clearly regards it as an essential part of the story he is writing; not because the hero's passion is too strong to remain silent, but because as a writer trained in a certain way he cannot conceive of any passion being silent. The term 'gratuitous' clarification applied by Erwin Panofsky to the scholastic *manifestatio* is equally true of this and many other early monologues. Their aesthetic justification came later, when they were already in existence as a recognized form of literary expression. In the five

[1] Cf. Omer Jodogne, 'Le caractère des œuvres antiques aux XIIᵉ et XIIIᵉ siècles', in *L'Humanisme médiéval dans les littératures romanes du XIIᵉ au XIVᵉ siècle* (Paris, 1964), 79: 'Par cette découverte d'une forme heureuse de l'analyse, l'auteur d'*Enéas*, du début à la fin de son œuvre, a fait franchir au roman une étape décisive. Je crois que c'est notre écrivain qu'on pourrait appeler le créateur du roman français. De narrateur, il est devenu romancier.'

[2] *Le Roman de Troie*, ed. L. Constans, Société des Anciens Textes Français (Paris, 1904–12), ll. 17638–746. Achilles is still silent in Dares who confines himself to the remark that having seen Polyxena Achilles fell violently in love with her and lived from then onwards in the odium of a consuming passion.

[3] *De Excidio Trojae Historia*, ed. F. Meister (Leipzig, 1873), ch. xxvii.

verse romances of Chrétien de Troyes, written between 1165 and 1181,[1] the monologue often serves as the focus of the entire action of the story. The story of Cligès and Fénice is prefaced by that of the hero's parents, Alexandre and Soredamors. Alexandre, the son of the Emperor of Byzantium, drawn by the fame of King Arthur's court, enters King Arthur's service at Winchester and accompanies him across the sea to Brittany. On this journey he meets King Arthur's niece Soredamors who until then had despised love. But she is soon punished for her pride: the moment she sees Alexandre, elegant, handsome, noble in every thought and gesture, their glances meet, love makes them his captives, and they struggle in vain against his power. In a long monologue Soredamors reveals every wavering thought that passes through her mind, drawing her inspiration from Ovid's *Metamorphoses* and freely echoing the monologues of Pomona, Medea, and Thisbe.[2] Alexandre's passionate soliloquy is conceived in a similar fashion. 'I feel', he exclaims, 'that my illness is too grievous to be healed by any medicine or draught, by any herb or root. For some ills there is no remedy, and mine lies so deep that it cannot be treated[3]. . . And yet', he adds,[4] 'I do not know what disease this is which has me in its grip, and I know not whence this pain has come. I do not know? I think I know full well: it is Love that causes me this pain. How is that? Can Love do harm? Is he not gentle and well-bred? I used to think that there was naught but good in Love; *mes je l'ai molt felon trové.*' Finally he resigns himself to his fate:

Now let Love do what he will with me as with one that belongs to him, for I wish it and it pleases me. Let not this malady leave me; I would rather it always maintained its hold and that health never came to me save from the source that causes the disease.[5]

---

[1] This is the traditional dating, still accepted by some critics, but seriously questioned by others who prefer to place the composition of Chrétien's romances some five years later. Cf. Stefan Hofer, 'Alexanderroman — Erec und die späteren Werke Kristians', *Zeitschrift für romanische Philologie*, lx. 245–61; Anthime Fourrier, 'Encore la chronologie des œuvres de Chrétien de Troyes', *Bibliographical Bulletin of the International Arthurian Society*, ii. 69–88; Jean Misrahi, 'More Light on the Chronology of Chrétien de Troyes', ibid. xi. 89–120; Rita Lejeune, 'La date du *Conte del Graal* de Chrétien de Troyes', *Moyen Âge*, lx. 56 ff.; and H. and R. Kahane, 'L'énigme du nom de Cligès', *Romania*, lxxxii. 113–21.

[2] *Cligès*, ed. Micha, ll. 454–515. [3] Ibid., ll. 638–44. [4] Ibid., ll. 656–63.
[5] Ibid., ll. 857–64.

Gaston Paris thought that all this was out of place in the story because Alexandre and Soredamors had no reason to fear any obstacle to their happiness: the son of an emperor and the niece of a king need have no hesitation in declaring their love to each other and to the world at large; admirably matched as they are, they can dispense with heart-searchings and contemplate marriage as a matter of course.[1] The error here is one which is by no means confined to nineteenth-century 'realistic' criticism: it is still being perpetrated almost daily by critics who judge medieval writings by their own standards of *vraisemblance*. Chrétien's object was not to tell us how such things normally happen, but to make a very simple story into one which develops simultaneously on two levels: that of feeling and that of action, one constantly motivating the other, even when by realistic standards no such motivation is required. It is not contemporary morals or proprieties that dictate the structure and composition of the romance, but the feeling that certain ways of presenting even the most straighforward issues are part of the kind of artistry that the reader expects and enjoys.

A later critic, Myrrha Borodine, in her fine analysis of the poem, suggests that in this case the absence of external obstacles is, on the contrary, part of the psychological situation which Chrétien endeavours to portray: 'The conflict is within the lovers' hearts, not outside them, and Chrétien's art consists in revealing to us a world of duties, scruples and delicate hesitations, which is the essence of courtly love.'[2] This is certainly true in the sense that from Chrétien's point of view there was room for scruples and hesitations in the lovers' minds no matter how favourable the circumstances in which they found themselves; but one should add that the reason why he found room for such things even in the most unlikely situations was not his desire to explore uncommon states of mind, but his determination to make the work structurally complete. The monologues of Alexandre and Soredamors are examples of interpretation accompanying and

[1] *Journal des Savants* (1902), 351.
[2] *La Femme et l'amour au XIIᵉ siècle d'après les poèmes de Chrétien de Troyes* (Paris, 1909), 94.

clothing a seemingly simple incident and thus providing it with a new dimension.[1]

When later on in the same work Chrétien has to describe how the hero comes to take leave of the heroine, Fénice, prior to his departure for the court of King Arthur, Chrétien makes him say: 'It is right that I should ask leave from you to whom I altogether belong',[2] and the poet adds that although many a secret sigh and sob marked the scene, the eyes of none were keen enough, nor the hearing sharp enough, to learn from what they said that there was any love between Cligès and Fénice. This does not prevent Fénice's thoughts from going back to the scene. She 'takes on her tongue', as Chrétien puts it, 'instead of spice, a sweet word which for all Greece she would not wish Cligès to have used in any sense other than that in which she understood it when he first uttered it'. Cligès had said that he was 'altogether hers'. This word 'she takes into her mouth and heart to be all the more sure of it . . . She strives to find and hold some ground on which to stand . . .' With what intention did Cligès say 'I am altogether yours'? Was it love that prompted him? Fénice is far from certain that this was really so, and the interior monologue—one of the first on record—goes on for well over a hundred lines, disclosing further doubts and hesitations in the heroine's mind.

This is 'interlinear' commentary. Nothing like it is to be found in the literature of medieval Europe before the middle of the twelfth century; but to us, eight hundred years after it was written, it seems so familiar that we can hardly imagine an age when such things were unknown. It is *our* language that Fénice speaks when she embarks upon her minute analysis of the simple words spoken by Cligès. And it is again *our* language that Chrétien speaks when on another occasion, in his most famous romance, *Lancelot*, he analyses his hero's behaviour. The facts of the story are simple. In an attempt to rescue Guinevere from captivity Lancelot loses his horse and has to face the choice between failure and utter disgrace. As he walks in his heavy armour he meets a dwarf driving

---

[1] This is what W. P. Ker who, not inexcusably, seems to have misunderstood the situation much in the same way as Gaston Paris did before him, calls 'a sudden and annoying change to the common impertinences of the amatory professional novelist' (op. cit., p. 352).   [2] *Come a celi cui je suis toz* (l. 4327).

a cart and cries out: 'Dwarf, tell me if you have seen my lady the queen pass by.' And the dwarf replies: 'If you will get up into the cart you will hear by to-morrow what has happened to the queen.' A cart in those days, Chrétien tells us, was never used except for criminals, and whoever was put in a cart lost all honour and was never afterwards welcomed in any court. So Lancelot hesitated, but only for two steps, before getting in. This is the story, or at least the main part of it. And here is the commentary:

It was unlucky for him that he shrank from the disgrace and did not jump in at once, for he later regretted the delay. Reason, which is inconsistent with the dictates of love, bids him refrain from getting in, warning him and counselling him not to do or undertake anything for which he may reap shame and dishonour. Yet reason which dares thus speak to him reaches only his lips, not his heart; for love is enclosed within his heart bidding him and urging him to mount at once upon the cart. So he jumps in, since love will have it so, feeling no concern about the shame: he is prompted by love's commands.

Thus an incident which, the poet tells us, did not last more than a second or two—the space of Lancelot's two steps—is made the subject of a disquisition in which the problem of the relative importance of love and honour, of duty to chivalry and duty to the lady, is raised in all its daunting complexity. The subtle balance between the two duties, between the dictates of reason and the dictates of love, is what motivates both the hero's hesitation and his action, just as later on in the story a somewhat different balance between the same conflicting principles of conduct will motivate the scene in which, to Lancelot's distress, Guinevere will rebuke him: not for having disgraced himself, but for having hesitated to do so. The narrative proper will not be devoid of interest; but it will matter little compared to its increasingly more subtle and systematic elucidation, just as in contemporary, or slightly later, polyphony—in the work of Léonin's successor, Perrotin, in the three-part counterpoint or *organum triplum*—the complexity of the upper parts will be matched by the diminishing importance of the *cantus firmus*.

This same work—the 'story of the cart'—can serve as an example of the other—the rhetorical type of elaboration. Lancelot's adventures on the way to the castle where Guinevere is held captive, the exploits he performs on her behalf, her release from captivity, her attitude to Lancelot, and his distress at her displeasure are all related to a particular conception of courtly love, which was perhaps not Chrétien's own, but which he adopted here as a means of showing how these various episodes of the story could be arranged and presented if human behaviour were governed by the extreme form of courtly service. In his attempt to rescue Guinevere Lancelot sacrifices his knightly honour: he humbly submits to being driven in a cart—a symbol of public disgrace. And yet, in spite of this, and in spite of all his feats of bravery, he is rebuked by Guinevere because she knows that before getting into the cart he paused 'for two steps'; even this momentary hesitation between his duty to her and his honour was, she thought, an offence against courtly love. In *Yvain* the courtly theme appears in a less rigid form. Yvain is persuaded to join the company of Arthur's knights and leave his lady, Laudine, who lets him go provided that he will return at the end of the year. He is filled with grief. 'The king can take his body away; but over his heart he has no power, for his heart remains attached to her whom he leaves behind, and no one can remove it from her.'[1] And Yvain goes on to say that a year would be too much: he could never stay away so long. The irony of it is that he does. The excitement of the adventure gets into his blood, and this is precisely what gives point and substance to his monologue on the eve of his departure. What Chrétien wants us to know and to feel is not simply that Yvain forgot his lady, but how it comes about that the deepest feelings in a man's heart are eclipsed for a time under the stress of circumstances: a state of things which in our own century has been called *les intermittences du cœur*. As a recent critic puts it: 'It is the story of a knight who lost the favour of his *dame* through pride and neglect of his duty, but who won her back by humility,

[1] ll. 2642–6:

> Li rois le cors mener an puet,
> Mes del cuer n'an manra il point;
> Car si se tient et si se joint
> Au cuer celi qui se remaint,
> Qu'il n'a pooir que il l'an maint.

faith in God and the right, and careful attention to his duties as a good knight.'[1] Our attention is constantly directed not so much to the details of Yvain's adventures, nor even to the fact of his apparent disloyalty towards Laudine, but to the motives behind the visible action of the story. The narrative remains continuous on both levels: that of the meaning and that of the matter, and the two 'voices' are heard simultaneously throughout.

All this is not to say that it is permissible for us to classify Chrétien's romances as examples of psychological realism in the modern sense of the term. Chrétien lets the characters enact a line of argument that happens to interest him, no matter what kind of characterization, real or unreal, may emerge as a result.[2] He certainly would not have understood Hugh Walpole's remark to the effect that the character in any novel 'should have existed before the book that reveals it to us began and should continue after the book is closed'.[3] The world of fiction is to him an essentially literary world, almost as remote from the 'portrayal of people' as the animal ornament of the Romanesque period was from any likeness to real living creatures. This does not exclude occasional touches of realism in the description of the characters' behaviour, any more than the stylized animal ornament excludes an occasional likeness to real animals.[4] But it would be misleading to say that Chrétien's purpose in introducing such characters as Enide, Fénice,

---

[1] Julian Harris, 'The Rôle of the Lion in Chrétien de Troyes' *Yvain*', *Publications of the Modern Language Association of America*, lxiv (Dec. 1949), no. 5, p. 1163.

[2] The notion of 'portraying' people is as alien to his mind as the modern sense of perspective to the pictorial vision of his contemporaries. There is, of course, a sense in which even in a modern context 'life' and 'people' can never be anything more than a means of sustaining a chosen formal medium. The assumption that it is the main business of any writer to create characters 'drawn from life' stems in English criticism from a traditional fallacy traceable to the eighteenth century. It was brilliantly exposed over thirty years ago by Professor L. C. Knights in *How Many Children had Lady Macbeth?* (reprinted in *Explorations* in 1946) and more recently by Walter Kaufman in his essay 'Goethe versus Shakespeare', *Partisan Review*, no. 6 (Nov.–Dec. 1952), 621–2, 625–9.

[3] *The Waverley Pageant*, p. 38. Quoted by L. C. Knights, op. cit., p. 1.

[4] Cf. Wilhelm Worringer, *Form in Gothic*, authorized tr. ed. Herbert Read (London, 1927), 60: 'The animal ornament is not the result of a direct observation of nature: it is composed of imaginary shapes, evolved more or less arbitrarily from the linear fantasy, and without which they do not exist. It is a playing with memories of nature within the limits of this abstract linear art, without any aim of distinctness such as would be proper to the observation of nature.'

Lancelot, or Guinevere was to make them behave like 'real people': everything they do is related to a problem and its elaboration within the work, since it is with problems that courtly poetry is concerned, not with human realities. 'Life', even courtly life, is for Chrétien not a model, but 'a vast mass of potential literary forms',[1] only a few of which can materialize in the framework of a romance; and the choice is invariably related to the problem raised. The next stage in the development of 'character' brings us no closer to the realm of psychological realism. The habit of seeing in a story an expression of a meaning or theme naturally leads to the creation of personified meanings and themes which may behave as characters, although it is clear that they have no existence of their own. Indeed no good poet, so Dante tells us, would allow such a confusion to arise in the reader's mind, for 'it would be a shameful thing if one should rime under the cloak of a figure of speech or colour of rhetoric and afterwards, being questioned thereof, should be unable to strip one's words of such clothing and reveal their true meaning'.[2] The 'true meaning'—*verace intendimento*—is the sense concealed by the figure of speech, the thought behind what Dante calls 'figura o colore rettorico'—in this instance, Love represented as if it were not only an intelligent substance, but a *sustanzia corporale*.[3] The method used by Chrétien de Troyes thus leads naturally to the allegory of the *Romance of the Rose* and of the *Vita Nuova*, not to the 'story of character' as understood by modern realistic novelists. It is the first example in French literature of a *roman d'analyse* based not on observation but on reflection.

The themes of Chrétien's five romances are strikingly inconsistent with one another: they represent varying attitudes to such important 'doctrinal' issues as the courtly code of behaviour, the duties of a knight towards his lady and towards

---

[1] Northrop Frye, *Anatomy of Criticism*, p. 122.

[2] '. . . grande vergogna sarebbe a colui, che rimasse cose sotto vesta di figura o di colore rettorico, e poi domandato, non sapesse dinudare le sue parole da cotale vesta, in guisa ch'avessero verace intendimento' (*Vita Nuova*, xxv). The translation given above is an adaptation of Rossetti's, ed. H. Oelsner (London, 1908), 131–3. On this passage see C. S. Lewis, *Allegory of Love*, p. 47.

[3] '. . . non solamente sustanzia intelligente, ma si come fosse sustanzia corporale' (ibid).

knight-errantry, and the duties of the lady herself. The only constant feature is the practice of expressing through each story a particular point of view and conveying in this fashion several different facets of courtly feeling. The proper medium for a consistent expression of courtly ideology is lyric and allegorical poetry; romance by its very nature favours variety rather than consistency: ideas are there merely to show how the story could be adapted to them, and it is a merit, not a fault, in a poet like Chrétien to have shifted his ideological ground in passing from one romance to another. Ideologically he remained uncommitted even after he had produced his two *romans à thèse*, *Cligès* and *Lancelot*; as uncommitted as any artist would be who had no preoccupations outside his art. Claudel once said that he could not really tell what love meant to him as an author except that it was one of the devices ('un des engins') used in the composition of his plays.[1] For him as for Chrétien the work was a means of giving shape to amorphous matter and thought—of producing the desired relationship between events and their antecedents. It was a statement 'not of philosophy, but of an ordered emotion'.[2] The real novelty of romance was precisely this 'ordering' quality: the urge not merely to move and to impress, but to understand.

[1] Paul Claudel, *Mémoires improvisés recueillis par Jean Amrouche* (Paris, 1954), 309: 'Au point de vue de l'auteur dramatique que je suis, l'amour est surtout un des engins, un des principaux ressorts d'une action dramatique.' For an interesting Old French parallel to this use of *engin*, cf. *Roman de Troie*, l. 122, where it occurs in combination with *sen* ('Par son sen e par son engin'). Gottfried von Strassburg echoes this phrase when he speaks (*Tristan*, l. 33) of 'Chunst unde nâhe sehender sîn' ('artistic skill and the close-scrutinizing mind').

[2] L. C. Knights (op. cit., p. 29) uses this phrase to describe the art of tragedy as understood by Shakespeare.

III

TRADITION AND DESIGN

ANY thoughtful reader of medieval romance finds himself sooner or later faced with a dilemma not unlike that which confronts the traveller in a fairy-tale who comes to a crossroads: whichever way he may turn, not only dangers, but rewards and fairies lie ahead. He can turn one way and enter without any effort the enchanted realm of popular fancy; and as he travels along, at each step new vistas of magic lands will be revealed to him, new wonders and new mysteries. Or he can turn the other way and find himself following the tracks not of giants and magicians, but of the wielders of fine verse and prose, of masters of narrative art at its most delicate and most graceful; he will then follow the steep road that leads to the discovery of the 'shaping spirit of imagination'. Whatever he stands to gain in one direction he is apt to lose in the other; such has been the fate of many who have made the choice, whether they knew it or not.

Perhaps we have travelled too far already in one direction to be able to heed the warning; but if we feel any regret for what in other circumstances might have attracted and absorbed our attention, we ought to remember that for better or worse most medieval romance writers followed this same road. They who had all the wonders of the Isle of Britain at their command, and all the mysteries of Brocéliande to call them out, applied their minds to the art of composing long and spacious poems which, if we are to believe W. P. Ker, have more affinity to the 'heroic romance' of seventeenth-century France than to the dreams of Spenser and Coleridge. 'There is', he tells us, 'a disappointment prepared for anyone who looks in the greater romantic authors of the twelfth century for the music of the *Faerie Queene* or *La Belle Dame sans Merci*.'[1] Medieval 'magic' is found elsewhere: in the poems of

[1] *Epic and Romance*, p. 326.

Brynhild, in the tragic Sagas, in the English and Germanic ballads. Chrétien de Troyes and his contemporaries, who founded the genre so misleadingly called 'Romance', drew, of course, freely and indiscriminately upon the vast store of exotic traditions, written and oral; but faithful to the precepts of their native rhetoric, they were primarily interested in the way they handled their material, not in the material itself. They would have had some difficulty in following the remark once made by Jessie Weston to the effect that because 'the Arthurian legend has its roots in folk-tradition', 'the abiding charm of its literary presentment is due to the permanent vitality and pervasive quality of that folklore element'.[1] And nothing would have surprised them more than the great gulf fixed between those who believe that 'the roots of that goodly growth spring from myth and faery' and a later school which treats romance as an example of 'the conscious production of literary invention'.

An interesting indication of how twelfth-century poets viewed their own work and how they thought the reader should approach it is contained in the opening lines of Chrétien de Troyes's *Erec et Enide*. Speaking of himself in the third person Chrétien says:

Since in his opinion it is reasonable that everyone should always endeavour to speak well and teach the right things, Chrétien de Troyes draws ('tret') from a tale of adventure ('d'un conte d'avanture') a very fine *conjointure* ('une mout bele conjointure'), whereby it may be proved and made known that he is not wise who does not use his learning so long as God gives him grace.[2]

There are about as many renderings of the word *conjointure* as there are critics who have tried to explain it.[3] Chrétien's German

---

[1] Preface to *Guingamor, Lanval, Tyolet, Le Bisclaveret, Four Lais rendered into English Prose from the French of Marie de France and Others*, by Jessie L. Weston (David Nutt, London, 1900), xiv.

[2] *Erec et Enide*, ll. 9–18: 'Por ce dit Crestiiens de Troies / Que reisons est que totes voies / Doit chascuns panser et antandre / A bien dire et a bien aprandre, / Et tret d'un conte d'avanture / Une mout bele conjointure, / Par qu'an puet prover et savoir / Que cil ne fet mie savoir / Qui sa sciance n'abandone / Tant con Deus la grace l'an done.' *Abandoner* = 'make liberal use of'. Cf. ibid., line 6110.

[3] Much of what follows in this chapter was originally written as a paper for one of the annual general meetings of the Society for the Study of Medieval Languages and Literature. A free adaptation of these same pages will be found in ch. v of *A la Recherche d'une poétique médiévale*.

editor, Wendelin Foerster, gives in his Glossary three renderings: *Verbindung* ('connection'), *Vermutung* ('conjecture'), and *Schluß-folgerung* ('chain of reasoning', 'argument'), but favours the last as being the most appropriate.[1] He refers to the *Miracle de St. Éloi* where *conjointure* is used in the sense of 'inference';[2] but what the author of this work has in mind is the method of interpreting the movement of the stars, and the text is in any case about a century later than Chrétien's *Erec*.[3] Before *Erec* there is no example of the word in twelfth-century French. The situation is one which some critics find challenging in that it provides ample room for conjecture and no apparent means of disproving even the least likely hypothesis. Foerster makes the word mean what he thinks it ought to mean in the context. Later critics, proceeding in exactly the same way, arrive with equal confidence at a variety of different meanings. Baist translates *conjointure* 'theme'—the theme of the sparrow-hawk, which Chrétien borrowed from his source (assuming that he had a source).[4] William Nitze thought it meant 'the combination of features or motifs taken from the source'[5]—a good guess, but still only a guess. Wilhelm Kellermann[6] and the Tobler–Lommatzsch Dictionary[7] suggest as an equivalent the German *Anlaß*—'occasion', 'opportunity', again without conclusive evidence.

[1] Two further meanings seem to have occurred to Foerster: *Ereignis, Vorfall* (*Erec*, p. 298) and *Kombination* (ibid., p. lxi): 'Er schält nur aus dieser Erzählung eine Kombination heraus, die ihm sehr gefallen ist.'

[2] Foerster omits to mention another example from the same text, quoted by Godefroy, 'Sans conjointure et sans defois', meaning 'without having to reason it out, to put two and two together, and without any difficulty'. Tobler–Lommatzsch's interpretation of the example quoted by Foerster is *Vergleichung der einzelnen Umstände*, which is not the same as *Schlußfolgerung*.

[3] In the chronicle of Philippe Mousket *conjointure* means 'grammatical construction': 'On doit escrire les figures / Et asambler les conjointures' (ed. F. de Reiffenberg (Bruxelles, 1837–8)).

[4] 'Die *bele conjointure* . . . ist aller Wahrscheinlichkeit nach weiter nichts als das Motiv von dem Sperber, der der Schönsten gehören soll.' Quoted by Foerster in his edition of *Li Conte de la Charrete*, p. lxxii.

[5] *Modern Philology*, xi (1913–14), 486–8. In an article in *Archiv für das Studium der neueren Sprachen und Literaturen* (clxviii, 48), R. R. Bezzola suggests a similar meaning (*jonction, composition*), but again without stating his grounds.

[6] *Aufbaustil und Weltbild Chrestiens von Troyes im Percevalroman*, Beiheft 88 zur *Zeitschrift für romanische Philologie* (Halle, 1936), 35. The work was published as a separate volume in 1968.

[7] *Altfranzösisches Wörterbuch*, s.v. *conjointure*.

One way of checking these suggestions is to replace the word in the semantic structure of twelfth-century French usage. We know that in Chrétien's time two related verbs were in current use: *joindre* and *conjoindre*, and we also know that *joindre* had produced the verbal noun *jointure*. Is it not reasonable to assume, then, that *conjointure*—whether coined by Chrétien or by someone else—arose, as words often do, as a means of completing an existing series, of filling a semantic vacuum? *Conjoindre* meant 'to link', 'to make a whole out of several parts'. The noun formed from this verb would presumably mean 'a whole made out of several parts' or simply 'arrangement'.[1] That this was in fact the case is confirmed by a piece of evidence of a different kind. In a well-known passage of Horace's *De Arte Poetica* poets are advised to use familiar material, because a great poet can make a work of art so perfect that 'if another made the same attempt he would sweat and toil in vain': such is the power of 'arrangement and composition'. The phrase Horace uses here is *series juncturaque*,[2] and earlier on he qualifies *junctura* by the adjective *callida*—'subtle', 'artfully devised'.[3] Since, as F. E. Guyer and, before him, William Nitze pointed out,[4] 'the prologue to *Erec* was largely inspired by Horace's *De Arte Poetica*', it is difficult to resist the conviction that when Chrétien used—or invented—the word *conjointure* he had in mind Horace's *junctura*, and that the phrase *bele conjointure* is modelled on *callida junctura*.

[1] This would also throw light on a curious late twelfth-century example quoted by Godefroy: 'Cele forme, cele peinture, / *Se Dieus n'i meist conjoincture* / *Tel com l'ame qui la governe,* / Fust ausi come la lanterne / Ou il n'a clarté ne lumiere' (Everat, *Bible*, MS. B.N. fr. 12457, f. 4ᵛ). I take the italicized words to mean: 'if God had not given it some such organizing principle as the soul which rules over it': a natural derivative from the meaning suggested above. The same literal meaning and some of its derivatives ('the action of joining together', 'the fact or state of being joined together'; 'a joining', 'conjunction', 'combination') are recorded in the O.E.D. as obsolete connotations of the English *conjuncture*, with examples from Walton (1665, 1672), Hobbes (1679), and Butler (1736). *Conjunctura* is found in Old Provençal in the sense of 'joining together of man and wife' (cf. Provenzaliches supplement Levy's *Wörterbuch*, i. 326).

[2] ll. 242–3:
        . . . tantum series juncturaque pollet,
        Tantum de medio sumptis accedit honoris.

[3] ll. 47–8:
        Dixerit egregie, notum si callida verbum
        Reddiderit junctura novum.

[4] *Romance in the Making* (New York, 1954), 62–3.

Chrétien here contrasts his own achievement with the performance of certain story-tellers who mutilate (literally: 'break into pieces') and spoil their material:

> Depecier et corronpre suelent
> Cil qui de conter vivre vuelent,[1]

and proudly asserts—following Horace's lead—that his work will last in people's memory for ever because, unlike those vulgar story-tellers—*conteors*—who earn their living by telling stories, he, Chrétien, will not fail to make good and generous use of his learning. This makes his meaning even clearer. It is, then, the art of *composition* in the etymological sense of the term that he seems to regard as the proper means of turning a mere tale of adventure into a romance,[2] and it is upon this delicate art, which only a learned man can practise properly, that he wants the reader to focus his attention. At the same time, however, he does not want us to forget that *conjointure* is merely a method of dealing with the material; it is not a substitute for the *conte*, but something which a skilful poet can and must superimpose upon it. One element is to be added to the other, and the poet would defeat his purpose if he tried to suppress one in favour of the other.

A poet's theory of the art of poetry is not necessarily true of his own work, but to test the validity of Chrétien's remarks it should suffice to examine one section of his *Erec et Enide*, the episode known as 'La Joie de la Cour'.[3] To arrive at some degree of clarity it might be useful to treat it, to begin with, as one treats a painting when its bare outline is being reproduced. Let us imagine that we have placed a piece of tracing paper over the canvas

---

[1] ll. 19–22, ed. Foerster:

> D'Erec, le fil Lac, est li contes,
> Que devant rois et devant contes
> Depecier et corronpre suelent
> Cil qui de conter vivre vuelent.

[2] This interpretation seems to have occurred to Mario Roques. In the introduction to his edition of *Erec et Enide* (p. vi) he uses the phrase 'ensemble cohérent et organisé'. Unfortunately he qualifies it in such a way as to suggest the technique of modern drama rather than that of a medieval romance: 'un ensemble . . . *que créent ou du moins dirigent ou infléchissent des caractères*, et qui prend, de ce fait, une signification, une valeur d'exemple'. The italics are mine.

[3] *Erec et Enide*, ed. Mario Roques, ll. 5319–6358; ed. Foerster, ll. 5367–6 410.

and that we are only trying to sketch in the main features of the original design—the shape and the arrangement of its component elements. Seen in such fashion the episode of 'La Joie de la Cour' would be something like this:

> To prove his devotion to his lady a knight called Mabonagrin has promised to remain with her in an orchard until he has been defeated in single combat. She thinks that he will never suffer defeat and therefore never leave her. Mabonagrin proves invincible until he is challenged by Erec, his eighty-first opponent, who succeeds where all the others have failed. For Mabonagrin defeat means freedom: Erec's victory releases him from his vow and he returns to Court.[1]

Those who know the text will notice that this is by no means the whole story, and that what Chrétien says is much more complicated. I have deliberately reduced his account to a coherent and straightforward sequence of events, and the interesting thing is that in this form the story turns out to be a characteristically 'chivalric' episode, controlled on the one hand by the theme of *obedience to a vow*, and on the other by the device of *dramatic suspense*. As a courtly knight, Mabonagrin must remain faithful to the promise he has given to a lady; and again as a knight he is capable of producing dramatic surprises, inasmuch as one never knows whether a knight is going to defeat his opponents or be defeated by them. Such in a romance of chivalry is his true function: indeed, the whole mechanism of a romance depends for its proper working upon the unpredictable nature of chivalric combats and the equal chances of victory and defeat.

If we now go back to Chrétien's text, remove the tracing paper from its surface, and look at every detail of the canvas, the result will be somewhat disconcerting. We shall find Erec riding with Enid and Guivret and approaching a strongly fortified town built on an island in the middle of a deep, roaring torrent. Erec is told that none of the knights who have visited the island has come back; they have all perished in a perilous adventure called

---

[1] This summary follows closely the one given by M. Jean Fourquet in an article entitled 'Le rapport entre l'œuvre et la source chez Chrétien de Troyes et le problème des sources bretonnes', *Romance Philology*, ix (W. A. Nitze Testimonial), 298–312. I am indebted to this article for much of what I have to say about Chrétien's understanding of his task both in *Erec* and in the *Conte del Graal*.

'La Joie de la Cour'. That night Erec and his companions are lavishly
entertained by King Eurain to whom the town belongs, and the
next morning Erec is shown a garden outside the town. The
garden is surrounded by an invisible wall: a wall of air, as secure
as if it were of iron. It is an enchanted garden where the fruit is
always ripe and the flowers are always in full bloom, and every
bird sings that can gladden the heart of man. Whoever wished
to pick the fruit and carry it away with him would never find his
way out until he had restored the fruit to the tree. But as Erec
rides he sees a long row of stakes, each impaling a man's head,
except the last which supports only a blast horn. He is told that
this last stake is for the next victim's head, which may well be his,
and that no one has yet succeeded in blowing the horn. As he
follows the path he sees a beautiful woman lying on a silver bed
beneath a sycamore. A tall knight appears wearing red armour
and challenges him. After a long and fierce struggle the knight
surrenders and tells Erec his story: he had pledged his word to his
mistress never to leave the garden until he had been defeated in
single combat. The heads on the stakes are those of the men he
killed against his will. Now that he has been defeated and released
from his vow all those of the court will rejoice—hence the name
given to this adventure: 'La Joie de la Cour'. As Erec blows the
horn, which is so made that only the victor can sound it, the spell
is broken and all rejoice except the fairy mistress who has lost
her power over her captive.

Modern critics have found little to commend in this tale.
Gaston Paris thought it uninteresting, meaningless, and incoherent:
'Il est assurément impossible d'imaginer quelque chose de plus
absurde, de plus incohérent, et en même temps de moins intéressant
que ce récit, allongé d'ailleurs par le poète à grand renfort de
détails inutiles et raconté avec une fatigante prolixité.'[1] Those
who find delight in the vagaries of romantic fancy will be surprised
and shocked at these strictures, not realizing perhaps that Gaston
Paris is merely applying to *Erec* the traditional standards of modern
criticism. He looks for the 'logic' of the story and naturally fails
to find it. Why all these extraordinary details—the wall made of

[1] *Romania*, xx (1891), 154.

air, the magic horn which only responds to the victorious knight, the fruit that is always ripe, the strange fairy mistress who holds the place spell-bound? What have these things to do with an otherwise simple and straightforward chivalric episode? Some scholars have, of course, seized upon these supernatural traits in the endeavour to discover behind them either some profound universal symbolism or a fully developed Celtic tradition, and have made much of certain parallel traits in the *Mabinogion*: Mabon, son of Modron, was held captive in Caer Loyw, the Shining Fortress, below which ran a salmon river. The fortress was the abode of the sorceress who schooled Peredur in the use of arms. The magic horn belongs to another *Mabinogion* character, Bran the Blessed, whose supernatural feasts were held in a fair palace on the isle of Gwales. The fairy orchard is, of course, the Celtic Other-world, and the fairy mistress its queen.

Granted that all these things have either a symbolic value as part of what Bezzola calls 'la grande aventure de la vie', or a precise meaning and purpose in Celtic folklore, how is it that they have no such meaning and no recognizable purpose in Chrétien's romance? The usual answer is that they were imperfectly trans-mitted, and R. S. Loomis even thought that by discovering the accidents of transmission we could 'relieve Chrétien of respon-sibility for the faults of construction and the lapses in coherence to which otherwise he would have to plead guilty'.[1] But does Chrétien need this kind of defence? What poet worthy of that name would accept it? And does our humble status of interpreters justify us in trying to do more than explain the apparent 'faults of construction' and 'lapses in coherence' as part of the poet's design?

These faults and lapses may offend our logic; they do not necessarily offend his or that of any twelfth-century romance writer. The lady of the orchard is, on the chivalric plane, a courtly lady, a cousin of Erec's wife, Enid; on the mythological or tradi-tional plane she rules the kingdom of the Otherworld with all its enchantments. When Erec blows the horn he gives the con-ventional chivalric signal of the liberation of a stronghold by a

---

[1] *Arthurian Tradition and Chrétien de Troyes* (New York, 1949), 6.

victorious knight; but the horn is also a 'faery' object destined
for the chosen man. The pledge granted to the lady is part of the
normal etiquette of courtly love: but it is also an expression of
the supernatural power wielded by the fairy mistress. And the
final defeat of Mabonagrin is both part of the logic of chivalry
and part of the illogical sequence of events one expects in a fairy-
tale. The whole story is conceived, as it were, on two distinct
levels: that of the *conte d'aventure* and that of the *conjointure*, the
latter being the courtly pattern evolved from the former. The
two are developed on parallel lines, but while on the courtly
level the coherence of the story is above reproach, on the mythological level there is simply no need for any coherent sequence:
incidents occur and magical objects appear at random, no matter
where they come from or what their original significance may
have been. To look for some co-ordinated system of symbols in
Chrétien's use of such incidents and objects would be even less
profitable than to explain in allegorical terms the confused legendary
matter of *Orlando Furioso*. The cohesion of parts, the relevance of
detail, and the harmonious planning of narrative structure are
essential for the romance, not for the *conte*, which can remain as
depecié as it had been, according to Chrétien, in the hands of
ignorant story-tellers. The skilled poet is the one who takes it
up with a smile—a smile 'half of amusement, half of affection,
like a man returning to something that had charmed his childhood'.[1] Boiardo and Ariosto deal with their infinitely more chaotic
contes in much the same way, but at an accelerated tempo, un-
afraid of the orgy of adventures and the wild succession of
inexplicable characters.

The modern reader resents such liberties; he expects all the
main elements of a narrative composition to be co-ordinated and

[1] C. S. Lewis, *Allegory of Love*, p. 299. The comparison is used to describe the
point of view of the 'literary poets who take up the extravagances of popular romance'
and find in them a pleasure which is 'not only the pleasure of mockery'. Even
while they laugh at such things, 'the old incantation works'. Cf. Ernest Hoepffner's
remark in his article 'Matière et sens dans le roman d'Erec et Enide' (*Archivum
Romanicum*, xviii (1934), 438): 'Nous le voyons à l'œuvre, façonnant . . . quelque
aventure merveilleuse et mystérieuse, qui nous plonge en plein conte de fée, et que
Chrétien raconte avec un sérieux imperturbable, mais derrière lequel nous devinons
cependant le sourire amusé du conteur.'

has no patience with the duality and semi-obscurity of medieval romance, with the constant tension between *conte* and *conjointure*. A medieval romance writer, on the other hand, being both a *conteor* and a learned man well versed in the art of rhetorical adaptation, maintains quite naturally the incoherent fragments of a *conte*, or isolated traditional themes, while cultivating at a higher level a coherent courtly, or chivalric, narrative. John Steinbeck in *Tortilla Flat* comes very close to this conception of a novelist's task by balancing the 'picaresque' novel of adventure, which is the outward and coherent facet of the work, with the theme of the search for treasure which, on his own admission, was inspired by memories of the *Quest of the Grail*. This supporting theme is no more integrated with the visible structure of his story than is the theme of the Other World with that of the capricious courtly lady in Chrétien's *Erec*. And so a feature historically understandable in Chrétien reappears in a novel of our own time, obeying no doubt the mysterious law of forms echoing each other in defiance of time and space.

M. Jean Fourquet, who alone among critics has so far noticed this feature of Chrétien's romances,[1] suggests that it might account for the diversity of interpretations placed upon Chrétien's most controversial work, *Li Conte del Graal*. The burning issue until now has been the significance of the Grail theme as conceived by Chrétien. Volumes have been written and are still being written on the probable form of the Grail story *before* Chrétien (assuming that there was such a story) and on his treatment and understanding of it. What did he make of the Fisher King, of the Grail procession, of the mysterious castle, of the Dolorous Stroke? Is the Grail to be explained in terms of a Nature ritual, or of Christian worship, or again of certain Welsh traditions clustering around the concept of a platter of plenty?[2] There is, of course, in Chrétien's story a vast substratum of traditional material, disjointed and often

---

[1] Op. cit. See esp. pp. 298 ff.

[2] The following are the most characteristic examples of the present-day interest in these matters: A. C. L. Brown, *The Origin of the Grail Legend* (Cambridge, Massachusetts, 1943); *Lumière du Graal, études et textes présentés sous la direction de René Nelli* (Paris, 1951); Jean Marx, *La Légende arthurienne et le Graal* (Paris, 1952); *Les Romans du Graal aux XIIe et XIIIe siècles* (Colloques internationaux du Centre National de la Recherche Scientifique (Paris, 1956)).

obscure: the mysterious object called *un graal*, the procession, the maimed king, the simpleton who fails to ask the right question at the right time; and there is also a chivalric romance which conforms to a carefully thought-out pattern: the pattern of a gradual and painful training for perfect knighthood. M. Fourquet would not go as far as this in contrasting the two levels of meaning: for him they are 'les deux niveaux de la *cohérence*', each coherent in its own way, and he leaves it to the experts to discover the coherence of the folklore element. I venture to think that there is no need to do this or indeed to assume that Chrétien aimed at 'coherence' at *both* levels. In the *Conte del Graal*, as in the 'Joie de la Cour' episode, the two elements exist side by side, each representing a certain level of *meaning*. Perceval's decision to join a company of knights against his mother's wishes, his mother's death, for which he blames himself, and his eagerness to undertake adventures are all reasons for his failure to do the right thing at the right time, and ultimately for his punishment. Such is the real and cogent motivation of the story, and the story itself is primarily that of a young knight's slow progress towards maturity. Occasionally a folklore theme is woven into it. An old knight warns Perceval not to be too talkative: 'Whoever talks too much', he says, 'often says things which he has cause to regret . . . I admonish you, dear friend, not to give tongue too freely':

> Por che, biaux amis, vos chastoi
> De trop parler.[1]

Perceval will remember this advice only too well, and when he sees the Grail procession pass him he will deliberately refrain from asking questions, thinking all the time of the 'preudome',

> Qui dolcement le chastia
> De trop parler.[2]

The recurrence of exactly the same phrase in two passages separated by over 1,600 lines of text is, of course, deliberate; it makes for the continuity of the theme of excessive obedience to a reasonable precept. A characteristic variant of the traditional *Dümmlingsmärchen*

---

[1] Chrétien de Troyes, *Le Roman de Perceval ou le conte du Graal*, ed. W. Roach (Paris and Lille, 1956), ll. 1655–6.
[2] Ibid., ll. 3295–6

is thus skilfully attached to the general pattern of Perceval's progress. More frequently, however, motifs belonging to what M. Fourquet describes as the 'non-chivalric world' are left to look after themselves, chief among them being the Grail episode. What exactly it stands for we shall probably never know,[1] but this is perhaps immaterial as long as the real centre of gravity can legitimately be placed elsewhere. To inquire further would be to violate Chrétien's design. We must have the courage to interpret the old knight's advice literally, as Perceval did, refrain from asking unnecessary questions, and understand the whole story in terms of the dichotomy of *conte* and *conjointure*, neither of which should be obscured or diminished by the presence of the other.

There is reason to believe that this dichotomy extended far beyond Chrétien's own work and that it represented something inherent in a particular type of narrative composition characteristic of its time. An interesting and hitherto virtually unnoticed example occurs in the romance of Tristan as preserved in twelfth-century texts. The three most important versions of the story are the poems of Béroul, Thomas, and Eilhart. It is generally agreed that the original poem, to which Béroul refers as the *estoire*, is more accurately represented in his and in Eilhart's rendering than in the more elaborate adaptation by Thomas, whose work was widely read and imitated both in and outside the French-speaking world. But there is one puzzling detail. All three poets tell us that the tragic love of Tristan and Iseult was caused by a magic potion. The potion was made by Iseult's mother for Mark and Iseult. Tristan and Iseult, while crossing the sea, drank it by mistake, and from that moment nothing but

---

[1] The most cogent theory so far put forward is that of the late Leonardo Olschki in his study of Chrétien's *Conte del Graal* published in the *Memorie dell' Accademia Nazionale dei Lincei, Classe di Scienze Morali, Storiche e Filologiche*, serie VIII, vol. x, fasc. 3 (Rome, 1961). But even though Olschki succeeds in deciphering the meaning of *some* of the occurrences in the Grail castle, he believes that 'the Grail procession, its various symbols and characters, the subtle psychological insights which reveal profound human experience both of maternal and profane love, all this and much besides is pure poetry and not folklore or erudition: original creation and not pedantic imitation. Any attempt to penetrate further into the secrets of a poet of passion and feeling is vain curiosity rather than enlightened criticism.' I quote from the English translation by J. P. Scott published by the Manchester University Press (*The Grail Castle and its Mysteries*, Manchester, 1966).

death could release them from its power. According to Eilhart, the potion was so made that at first those who drank it could not live apart; if they were separated for half-a-day, they would fall ill; if for a week, they would die; but after four years the strength of the potion would abate and the lovers could separate.[1] Béroul describes the effect of the potion in similar terms, limiting it to three years instead of four.[2]

Bédier thought that no such limitation could have been conceived by the author of the primitive Tristan romance; that the poet to whom we owe the world's greatest love story could not have reduced the function of the magic love-drink to a temporary intoxication—'cette pharmacie', as he once described it in a conversation. He admitted that this view was based on a certain notion of what a great poet could or could not do, but he thought that aesthetically the argument was strong enough to support the theory that in this particular instance the story as told by Béroul and Eilhart was a distortion of the original; and he confidently declared that any reconstruction of the latter should, so far as the love-potion theme was concerned, rely on Thomas, even though Thomas was otherwise the least reliable of the three *remanieurs*.[3] There must have existed, he concluded, between the original *estoire* on the one hand and Béroul and Eilhart on the other, a remodelled version compiled by a clumsy but ingenious adaptor who reproduced the *estoire* accurately except for this one trait. Having noticed that in the *estoire*, after the lovers' exile in the forest of Morois, Iseult returns to King Mark and Tristan enters the service of the King of Brittany, the adaptor thought that this could only

[1] Eilhart von Oberge, *Tristrant*, ed. Franz Lichtenstein (Straßburg, 1877):

> sie musten sich minnen
> mit allen iren sinnen
> die wîle daz sie lebetin:
> vîr jâr si abir phlegetin
> sô grôzir lîbe beide,
> daz sie sich nicht gescheidin
> mochtin einen halbin tag.

[2] Béroul, *Le Roman de Tristan*, ed. Muret (Paris, 1903, 1913, 1928), and Ewert (Oxford, 1939), ll. 2139–40:

> La mere Yseut, qui le bolli[t],
> A trois anz d'amistié le fist.

[3] *Le Roman de Tristan par Thomas*, publié par Joseph Bédier, t. ii (1905), 236–9.

have happened if the influence of the potion had abated, at least partially. Hence the device of limiting its effect so as to allow the lovers to part. Such ingenuity, in Bédier's view, was precisely what one would expect from a *remanieur*: to attribute it to the original poet would be to deny his greatness and reduce the work to the rank of a trivial anecdote.

If in this instance Bédier felt free to settle a question of fact by an argument based entirely on his own aesthetic judgement, it was because there was at that time no means of dealing with the problem in a more objective fashion. The original Tristan poem was supposed to have inspired four entirely independent works: the poems of Béroul, Thomas, Eilhart, and the French prose romance of Tristan. In two of these the efficacy of the love-potion was restricted, in the other two there was no limita-tion, and only 'reasons of taste' could therefore legitimately decide between them. Since then, however, it has been shown that the prose romance is not an independent witness and that it bears clear traces of the influence of Thomas's poem. This means that there are only three 'primary' derivatives and that, barring coinci-dence, the agreement of any two of them against a third must be regarded as decisive for the reconstruction of the original poem. Whatever the consequences for our assessment of the value of the work, the fact that the potion abates after a few years in both Béroul and Eilhart must henceforth be accepted as sufficient proof that it did so in the *estoire*.[1] How, then, are we to reconcile this simple fact with another equally obvious one, the 'greatness' of the original Tristan romance?

We judge 'greatness' by certain qualities which appear to us to be inseparable from the very existence of a work of art, such as unity, coherence, continuity, and equilibrium.[2] What was

[1] Cf. W. Golther, *Tristan und Isolde* (Leipzig, 1907), 100–1; Gertrude Schoepperle, *Tristan and Isolt, a Study of the Sources of the Romance* (Frankfurt and London, 1913), 76–7; her article in *Romania*, xxxix (1910) on *The Love Potion in Tristan and Isolt* (pp. 277–96), and my essay on *The Love Potion in the Primitive Tristan Romance* printed at Le Puy-en-Velay in 1924 and reproduced in *Medieval Studies in Memory of Gertrude Schoepperle* (Paris and New York, 1927).

[2] 'We' in this context would include even the most progressive among the critics of our time, such as René Wellek in his 'Mode of Existence of a Literary Work' (*The Southern Review*, Sping, 1942) and Cleanth Brooks in *The Well Wrought Urn* (New York,

repugnant to Bédier in the 'limited' version of the love-potion theme was its incongruity; the source and the symbol of eternal love could not, he felt, be 'limited' in any way without losing its significance. But can we be certain that this apparent fault was not something inherent in the form of narrative used by the author of the original Tristan romance? When Chrétien imposes the scheme of a *conjointure* upon a *conte* he does not necessarily resolve the resulting incongruities. Is it not legitimate to suppose that the first Tristan poet acted likewise? That he had set himself the task of 'drawing' from his material *une mout bele conjointure* in Chrétien's sense of the term? The main difference between them would be that the Tristan poet had tried to build his story upon a substratum of tradition more akin to feudal epic than to courtly romance. At least one of his models—*Girart de Roussillon*—belonged to the cycle known as *la geste des révoltés*.[1] This was a cycle concerned with the fate of feudal barons conscious of the allegiance they owed their overlord and yet unable to maintain it under the stress of their *desmesure*—the medieval equivalent of *hybris*.[2] What the Tristan poet set out to do was to adapt his tale to this pattern— a pattern fully developed not only in *Girart de Roussillon*, but in *Raoul de Cambrai*, *Gormond et Isembart*, and other twelfth-century poems. The theme which the Tristan romance shares with them all is that of a tragic conflict between vassal and overlord. In spite of the wrongs of which the overlord may be guilty, the vassal feels that he has committed an unheard-of crime in turning against the man to whom he is bound by ties even more sacred than those of Nature. In the Tristan romance this theme persists in spite of the presence of another, presumably much older one, that of the love-drink, the *vin herbé*; never does the magic of it, all-powerful though it is, remove the cause of Tristan's misfortune—his sense of allegiance to Mark. 'We love each other', he says to the hermit who

1947), 194–214 ('The Heresy of Paraphrase'). The latter suggests (p. 203) the formula of 'a pattern of resolved stresses'. This is exactly what a twelfth-century romance of the type I am here discussing is not. 'A pattern of unresolved stresses' would be considerably nearer the mark. Cf. H. H. Glunz, *Die Literaresthetik des europäischen Mittelalters* (Bochum, 1937), 569–70.

[1] Cf. E. S. Murrell, *Girart de Roussillon and the Tristan Poems* (Chesterfield, 1926).

[2] For a fully documented account of the main characteristics of this *geste*, see W. C. Calin, *The Old French Epic of Revolt* (Paris, 1962).

tries to make him repent, 'because of the potion we drank: *ce fut pechiez*;[1] and *pechiez* can mean either sin or misfortune, or possibly both.

Tristan is King Mark's nephew and vassal, bound to him by all the ties of kinship and feudal loyalty. He and Iseult live in a very different world from that in which human passion can obliterate and even abolish the claims of the social order to which all men belong. Far from ever challenging this order, Tristan, exiled from Mark's court, has no thought of escaping to a happier land—to his own country or to Iseult's. Instead they live like outcasts in the forest, unable either to yield to the hermit's entreaties or to throw off the bonds which make their life, in Béroul's words, *aspre et dure*.[2] The feudal law and the resulting sense of a breach of loyalty do more than prevent the powers of magic from sweeping everything aside: they frustrate those powers in a significant way. The logic of feudal revolt calls for ultimate surrender: Girart de Roussillon, like Tristan, at first refuses to repent, but in the end, broken-hearted, unable to challenge the law of God which he has offended and the authority of the king whom he has betrayed, submits and does penance for his sins.[3] And the same logic forces Tristan to surrender Iseult to Mark. 'God,' he exclaims, 'how my uncle would have loved me and cherished me if I had not offended so greatly against him . . . So now I cry to God the Lord who rules this world and beg Him to give me strength to yield back Iseult to King Mark.'

It was not until the poet came to describe the separation of the lovers that the difficulty of reconciling it with the theme of the everlasting power of the love-drink became apparent to him. To solve it, to make the action on the supernatural plane coincide with the pattern of the feudal conflict, he limited the powers of the potion just enough to enable the lovers to live apart. 'My

[1] Béroul, ll. 1413-16:

> Il ne m'aime pas, ne je lui,
> Fors par un herbé dont je bui
> Et il en but: ce fu pechiez.

[2] Béroul, ll. 2170-1, 2185-8.
[3] *Girart de Roussillon, chanson de geste* publiée par W. Mary Hackett (Paris, 1953), ll. 7401-772.

lords, you have heard of the potion they drank which caused them to suffer for so long, but you do not know how long this love-drink, this potion was meant to last. Iseult's mother, who prepared it, made it for three years of love. She made it for Mark and her daughter. Another tasted it, and he it is who bears the pain of it.'[1] The logic of the supernatural has to give way to the logic of the feudal *conjointure*, for of the two levels of meaning, the super-natural and the human, it is the latter that seems paramount to the poet as it does to Chrétien de Troyes. Their point of view is the same; both are prepared to leave the legendary motif in its amorphous state, without any pretence at coherence, as long as they can combine it with a rationally planned composition which they claim as their own.

All this is not to say that the 'legend' had lost its appeal for the poet. There is ample evidence to the contrary. In Thomas the story ends with the lovers' death; the last lines of the poem tell us how Iseult, who arrived too late to save Tristan, died for sorrow.[2] In the original poem this was followed by an epilogue which has only survived in a late French manuscript (B.N. fr. 103) and in Eilhart.[3] The French text says that King Mark brought the bodies of Tristan and Iseult back to Cornwall and had their tombs built on the right and left of a chantry. But in one night there sprang from the tomb of Tristan a green and leafy briar. It climbed the chantry and took root again in Iseult's tomb. The people told the marvel to the king. Thrice did he command it to be cut down, but thrice it grew again as strong as before: such was the miracle of their love. Eilhart, who refrains here from mentioning Mark, speaks of the burial of the two lovers in one tomb, with a rose bush set over Iseult and a vine over Tristan, growing together so that they could in no wise be sundered. Whether or no this variant is genuine, Eilhart clearly echoes the words of the original poet

---

[1] Béroul, ll. 2133-46.
[2] *Le Roman de Tristan par Thomas*, ed. Bédier, ll. 3123-4:

> Tristrans murut pur sue amur,
> E la bele Ysolt pur tendrur.

[3] See Joseph Bédier, 'La mort de Tristan et Iseut', in *Romania*, xv (1886), 481-510.

when he says: 'It was the potion, so men told me, that did this thing.'[1]

Here, then, is the positive side of the dichotomy: the *conte* asserts itself in face of, and despite, the *conjointure*, as something which has a certain validity in the poet's eyes, no matter how many incoherences may result from it. Is it too much to suggest that this is precisely the way in which the Grail theme appealed to Chrétien de Troyes? He allows it to intrude upon his narrative because it has for him an attraction all its own. What more intriguing than Perceval's visit to the castle 'fairer than any this side of Beirut', where in a spacious square hall a grizzled man in purple and sable robes lies on a couch with four hundred men seated around him? And what a magnificent climax to this tale of mystery when Perceval sees a youth carrying a lance from the point of which a drop of blood flows down, and a beautiful damsel holding a *graal* in her hands, a vessel encrusted with precious stones and radiating a brilliant light! None of this is explained either directly or indirectly, and the subsequent adventures of Perceval and Gawain merely add to the mystery. Who are we to say that this is not precisely what Chrétien meant to happen?

If, as I believe, [says R. S. Loomis] Chrétien was a man of high intelligence, literary genius, and a more than elementary knowledge of religious matters, he could not have been satisfied with the inadequate motivation, the rambling plot, the strange moral emphasis, and the fantastically uncanonical representation of the Grail as a receptacle for the Host which we discover in his romance; far less could he have invented them.[2]

And so he concludes that Chrétien reluctantly followed 'through thick and thin' a work written by somebody else. It is true that Chrétien mentions a book about the Grail, which he says he received from his patron, Philip of Flanders; but nobody knows what that book contained, and the only reason for supposing that

---

[1] Op. cit., l. 9521: 'daz machte des trankes craft'. For a more detailed account of the significance of this theme in the primitive Tristan romance, cf. my contribution to *Tristan et Iseut à travers le temps* (Bruxelles, 1961) and pp. 86–104 of *A la Recherche d'une poétique médiévale*.

[2] Roger Sherman Loomis, *Arthurian Tradition and Chrétien de Troyes* (New York, 1949), 466.

it contained the entire matter of Chrétien's *Conte del Graal* is that in the opinion of some critics Chrétien was too great an artist and too intelligent a person to have produced such an absurd romance of his own accord. But when critics credit Chrétien with 'intelligence' and 'artistic sense', what do they do but equate *their* intelligence and *their* artistic sense with his? When Bédier condemned the love-potion theme as presented in Béroul's *Tristan*, or when Gaston Paris pointed disapprovingly to 'absurdities' and 'incoherences' in the 'Joie de la Cour' episode, they were both equally rash and equally unaware of their rashness, assuming—in strict conformity with an age-long tradition—that a good twelfth-century romance must satisfy the standards of 'goodness' which they consider valid.

To follow their lead would be to exclude from our aesthetic horizon more than just the early masterpieces of imaginative narrative. How, for instance, would *Moby Dick* stand up to their scrutiny? The spiritual theme of the story—its *conjointure*—is clear: it is a battle against evil conducted too long or in the wrong way; the white whale is the evil, and Captain Ahab is warped by constant pursuit until his knight-errantry turns to revenge. But how does this fit in with the rest, with what E. M. Forster calls 'the prophetic song' of the book, which 'flows athwart the action and the surface morality as an undercurrent'?[1] The obvious answer is that such things are not there to be 'fitted in' at all, any more than the enchanted orchard, or the Grail procession, or the love-potion.

It is in the next century that the 'fitting in' process will start in earnest. The varied and incoherent poetic legacy of the twelfth century will fall into carefully thought-out narrative sequences, missing links will be found, and a vast architectural design will emerge. The Perceval story will become the story of Galahad, the hero of a rigidly coherent *Queste del Saint Graal* in which every detail of the action will have its explicitly stated motive and no episode will be allowed to remain outside a carefully thought-out scheme. Similarly, in the thirteenth-century prose romance of Tristan the original dichotomy of the tale of magic and the tragic

[1] *Aspects of the Novel* (London, 1953 (pocket ed.)), 128.

tale of feudal loyalty will be resolved: Mark will become a villain and a traitor, and Tristan the hero, the legitimate champion of Iseult and of pure, triumphant chivalry. Not that the form discovered and practised by Chrétien de Troyes and his contemporaries will cease to exist. The art which leaves part of its material free from the restraints of design is still with us, concealed by new techniques and new skills; but it is the privilege of any reader of twelfth-century romance to see it in the making, to linger at the parting of the ways, and so unite in one perspective the two eternal facets of poetic fancy.

IV

THE WASTE LAND[1]

All that Nature did omit,
Art, playing second natures part, supplied it.
The Faerie Queene, iv. 8

IN his essay *The Anthropological Approach* published in 1962,
a year before his untimely death, C. S. Lewis wrote: 'It is either
in art, or nowhere, that the dry bones are made to live again.'[2]
The essay was a brilliant attack on 'the type of criticism which
always takes us away from the actual poem and the individual
poet to seek the sources of their power in something earlier and
less well known'.[3] Thus, according to Lewis, in dealing with
medieval romance the critics have been building round themselves
a second romance which is a distorted version of the first: 'a quest
story' in which the critic, not Perceval or Gawain, plays the
leading part. 'It is the critic who quivers at the surmise that everything he meets may be more important, and other, than it seemed.
It is to him that such hermits as Frazer and Miss Weston, dwelling
in the heart of the forest, explain the *significacio* of the ferlies.'
The real objection to their behaviour is, however, not that they
try to explain what we may have misunderstood, but that in the
process of explaining it they reject fiction as it was actually written.
They can 'respond to it only indirectly, when it is mirrored in
a second fiction, which [they] mistake for a reality'.[4] Behind this
disability lies the axiomatic belief that medieval literature had
constantly regressed from perfection to imperfection, from
coherence to incoherence, from logic to chaos—a belief which
persists today at all levels of scholarship, in spite of abundant

---

[1] This chapter is in the main an elaboration of an article published in *Medium
Ævum*, xxv. 175–80 ('The Dolorous Stroke'), and summarized in *A la Recherche d'une
poétique médiévale*, pp. 141–8.
[2] *English and Medieval Studies presented to J. R. R. Tolkien on the Occasion of his Seven-
tieth Birthday*, ed. Norman Davis and C. L. Wrenn (London, 1962), 223.
[3] Ibid., p. 224.　　　　　　　　　　　　　　　　　　[4] Ibid., p. 229.

evidence to the contrary: the romances of the thirteenth century
are still looked upon as 'mere rubble left over from some statelier
building'.[1] Recent research tends to show that the reverse is the
case;[2] that, as C. S. Lewis puts it, 'the romance is the cathedral
and the anthropological material the rubble that was used by
the builders'. This progressive approach is still in its pioneering
stage. It has been welcomed in some quarters,[3] but much still
remains to be done to secure its wider acceptance. At a conscious
level everybody will no doubt agree that literature is a constructive
rather than a destructive process; but it might be more difficult
to convince people that in the twelfth and thirteenth centuries,
more perhaps than at any other time in the history of narrative
art, the measure of artistry was the ability not to invent new
stories, but to build up sequences out of the existing ones. The aim
was not 'creation', in our sense, but re-creation—the elaboration
and transmission of inherited material. It was important 'to hand
on the matter worthily':[4] not worthily of one's own genius,
but of the matter itself.

All this is as much of a historical fact as the example of late
medieval architecture facing this page (Plate III): the inside view
of Genoa cathedral, which is the work of a northern French
architect. There are no fewer than twenty-four colonnettes placed
around an octagon, as if drawn together by some hidden force.
The parallel in literary history is the tendency to group together
stories or motifs which once existed as separate entities. In the

[1] There are, of course, a few welcome exceptions such as Robert Guiette's *Légende
de la Sacristine* (Paris, 1927), his edition of *Croniques et conquestes de Charlemagne* (Bruxelles,
1943), Jean Frappier's study of *La Mort le roi Artu* (Paris, 1936), and, among the
more recent publications, Fanni Bogdanow's *Romance of the Grail* (Manchester,
1966).

[2] C. S. Lewis, op. cit., p. 224. It was, I fear, wishful thinking on C. S. Lewis's
part to say in the same paragraph that the traditional type of criticism received a
'dolorous stroke' from an article of mine published under that title.

[3] Among others by Professor Jean Fourquet in his review of *Arthurian Literature
in the Middle Ages* (*Études anglaises*, xvi. 131). He calls it 'another Copernican revolu-
tion' and adds: 'Il n'est pas nécessaire d'être Merlin pour prédire que cette révolu-
tion remontera progressivement vers les origines.'

[4] C. S. Lewis, *The Discarded Image* (Cambridge, 1964), 211. He adds: 'If you had
asked Layamon or Chaucer "Why do you not make up a brand-new story of your
own", I think they might have replied (in effect) "Surely we are not yet reduced to
that"... The originality which we regard as a sign of wealth might have seemed to
them a confession of poverty.'

III. THE INTERIOR OF GENOA CATHEDRAL

Photograph Mansell Collection

twelfth century the story of Perceval and the Grail was never linked with that of Lancelot, and neither Lancelot nor Perceval had any place in the chronicles of Arthur's reign such as Wace's *Brut* or Geoffrey of Monmouth's *Historia*. From the point of view of Chrétien de Troyes those were entirely unrelated series of adventures, even though they were all connected with Arthur's court. The first attempt to bring them together was made by a later poet, Robert de Borron, a man 'endowed with boldness and piety, but with mediocre talent'.[1] His *Joseph* or 'the history of the Grail', followed by a *Merlin*, paved the way for the Arthurian cycle of romances which grew as a result of a further and more extensive use of the 'linking' process. The three initial themes—Lancelot, the Grail, and Arthur's reign—were first combined in such works as the *Perlesvaus*[2] and the *Didot-Perceval*,[3] but it was not until the 'Vulgate' Cycle of Arthurian romances had come into being between 1220 and 1225 that all sense of the separateness of these themes was lost. Something similar occurred in most branches of narrative literature, including the feudal and national epic. There was in all of them a constantly growing tendency towards coalescence.[4] An increasingly large number of hitherto independent narrative themes adhered to each other so as to form larger and more fully co-ordinated sequences. To visualize what this meant we need but remind ourselves of Charles Lamb's remark about Dr. Johnson's style which he greatly admired. 'Read one page of Johnson,' he wrote, 'you cannot alter one conjunction without spoiling the sense. In your modern books, for the most part the sentences in a page have the same connection with each other as marbles have in a bag; they touch without adhering.'[5]

[1] So described by M. Pierre Le Gentil in *Arthurian Literature in the Middle Ages, a Collaborative History*, ed. R. S. Loomis (Oxford, 1959), 251.

[2] Ed. William A. Nitze and T. Atkinson Jenkins, Chicago, 1932.

[3] Ed. William Roach (Philadelphia, 1941), who says that 'it would be appropriate to rename the romance . . . the *Prose Perceval*'.

[4] Cf. Jessie Crossland, *Medieval French Literature* (Blackwell, Oxford, 1956), 128: 'Perhaps it was the possibility of adding new stories, of reviving popular heroes and following them in their careers, of writing sequels and thus giving them a kind of cyclic character, which accounted for the immense popularity of these collections in the Middle Ages.' Some of the most interesting examples of this type of elaboration will be found in Dr. F. Bogdanow's *Romance of the Grail* (Manchester, 1965).

[5] Charles Lamb, *Critical Essays*, ed. William Macdonald (London, 1903), 270-1.

To illustrate the part played by the process of coalescence in the development of romance it should suffice to examine the evolution of a theme that runs through all the later forms of the Grail legend, whether English or French—the theme of the Waste Land. It is present in the minds of most modern poets concerned with the symbolism of the Grail; it is central to the work of both Charles Williams and T. S. Eliot. For these two poets, however, the Waste Land is a pre-literary myth which came into being *as a whole* before any Arthurian romance was written. Such references to the Waste Land as Arthurian literature contains are for them echoes of this half-forgotten legendary 'pattern' which a poet's imagination can perceive, if not reconstruct, in its entirety. T. S. Eliot gratefully acknowledges his debt to Jessie Weston's 'reconstruction': 'Miss Weston's book', he writes, 'will elucidate the difficulties of the poem much better than my notes do; and I recommend it (apart from the great interest of the book itself) to any who think such elucidation of the poem worth the trouble': for 'not only the title, but the plan and a good deal of the incidental symbolism of the poem were suggested' by this book. This is one of the rare cases in literary history where (barring irony on the poet's part) a work of scholarship has inspired a poem; but what made such a thing possible was not simply Eliot's high regard for the work, but his conviction that it contained a record of something which had once existed. Jessie Weston's *From Ritual to Romance* was to him what the Iliad was to Giraudoux when he wrote *La Guerre de Troie n'aura pas lieu*: a narrative of a myth or a legend recovered from the distant past. What if he were mistaken? What if Jessie Weston and all those who followed her were wrong in thinking that they could prove the existence of such a myth in pre-literary times on the sole basis of the extant literary works? Should we not then be justified in paying more attention to these works and less to what is supposed to lie behind them?

A simple thematic analysis of the Waste Land story will show that it consists of four main elements which occur in many different combinations: a miraculous weapon (a lance or a sword), a wound inflicted upon a king or a knight (the Dolorous Stroke, or, as

Charles Williams calls it, the 'Dolorous Blow'), the devastation
of the land, and finally the healing of the wound. The earliest text
in which any of these motifs occur is Chrétien's *Conte del Graal*
written in 1180 or 1181. There we find a king grievously wounded,
a miraculous weapon, and the land laid waste. But the three
motifs are not linked together in anything like a coherent sequence.
One of them—the motif of the 'maimed king'—is part of the
Perceval story proper. Perceval sees an old man lying on a couch
in a crowded hall in the castle[1] and is told afterwards that it is the
Fisher King who has been wounded through the thighs in battle:

> S'an est ancor si angoisseus
> Qu'il ne puet sor cheval monter.[2]

In a still later passage we are told that Perceval's failure to ask the
question he was expected to ask had prolonged the king's agony
and inflicted untold misfortunes upon the entire land:

> Dames en perdront lor maris,
> Terres en seront escillies
> Et puceles desconsillies,
> Qui orfenines remandront,
> Et maint chevalier an morront.[3]

This, however, is only a prefiguration of the Waste Land theme
proper which Chrétien will introduce in connection with one of
Gawain's adventures. An anonymous character will predict to
Gawain that the kingdom of Logres will be laid waste by a
mysterious lance:

> Et c'est escrit qu'il iert une hore
> Que toz li roiaumes de Logres,
> Qui jadis fu la terre as ogres,
> Sera destruis par cele lance.[4]

There is nothing in Chrétien's text to suggest that this evil lance—
'the lance of vengeance'—is the one which Perceval saw in the
Grail castle.[5] Hence there is no link between the Waste Land

[1] Chrétien de Troyes, *Le Roman de Perceval ou le Conte du Graal publié d'après le ms.
fr. 12576 de la Bibliothèque Nationale* par William Roach (Droz, Paris, 1956), ll. 3083–95.
[2] Ibid., ll. 3507–15.　　　[3] Ibid., ll. 4679–82.　　　[4] Ibid., ll. 6168–71.
[5] Cf. W. A. Nitze's remarks in 'Le Bruiden, le Château du Graal et la lance qui
saigne', in *Les Romans du Graal* (Colloques internationaux du Centre National de la

described in the above four lines and the motif of the Maimed King,[1] and no reason to suppose that any such link existed in Chrétien's mind. And since his method of adaptation consisted, as he himself claims, in adding rather than removing connections—his *conjointure* means precisely that—the tradition that preceded him must have been even less fully co-ordinated than his own version of the Waste Land theme.

It is not until we come to the 'First Continuation' of *Perceval* that a proper connection is established between the *terre gaste* and the Maimed King. A mysterious weapon is found lying broken upon the body of a dead man, and when Gawain sees it and asks the right question about it, the land regains part of its fertility. For, as we are told in the same passage, this weapon has destroyed

> Maint duc, maint prince, maint baron,
> Mainte dame, mainte pucele,
> Et mainte gentil damoisele.

The author then goes on to say:

> Bien avez oï longuement
> Parler del grant destruiement
> Par coi nos somes chi venu:
> Li roialmes de Logres fu
> Destruis, et toute la contree,
> Par le cop que fist ceste espee.[2]

Recherche Scientifique (Paris, 1956), 290–3), which seem to me to remain valid in spite of the objections raised by M. Jean Marx in his *Nouvelles Recherches sur la littérature arthurienne* (Paris, 1965), 174 ff.

[1] The *Perlesvaus* contains an elaboration of the passage in Chrétien connecting Perceval's failure to ask the 'unspelling' question with the misfortunes which befell the entire kingdom: 'Si s'aparut a lui li sainz Grauuz e la lance de coi la pointe de fer saine, ne ne demanda de coi ce servoit, ne cui on en servoit; por ce qu'il ne le demanda, sont totes les terres de guerre escommeües, ne chevaliers n'e[n]contre autre en forest q'il ne qeure sus e ocie s'il puet' (ed. Nitze, p. 38). This is still not the 'blighted land' theme proper, any more than the paraphrase of this same sentence on p. 50. The *Perlesvaus* is dated by its editor 'before 1212', 'presumably soon after 1200' (vol. ii, p. 189). In the *Didot-Perceval* (ed. W. Roach (Philadelphia, 1941)), a still earlier work, the episode appears characteristically in an even less developed form: 'quant il [Perceval] avra demandé que on en fait et cui on en sert de cel Graal . . . charont li encantement qui hui cest jor sont en le terre de Bretagne' (p. 151).

[2] *The Continuations of the Old French* Perceval *of Chrétien de Troyes*, vol. i, *The First Continuation* (*MSS. TVD*), ed. W. Roach (Philadelphia, 1949), ll. 13500–8. Cf. also ll. 13358–72 for another reference to the land being laid waste and ll. 13558 ff. for a description of the 'unspelling' effect of the question asked by Gawain: 'Et la terre en resoit peuplee / Qui par vos et par ceste espee / Est si destruite et essillie.' The

The last three lines are clearly a development of Chrétien's *li roiames de Logres . . . sera destruiz par cele lance*, now combined with the story of the fatal wound.

The process of coalescence continues in the Arthurian 'Vulgate' Cycle. In the *Queste del Saint Graal*[1] the same three motifs are found at first as in the First Continuation of *Perceval*: a king is killed by a magic sword and the stroke—now called 'the dolorous stroke'— causes the devastation of the land.[2] Then another variant occurs: a king is wounded by a magic weapon;[3] his wound does not cause the land to be laid waste, but a miraculous healing is promised by Perceval's sister who says to Galahad: 'he will not be cured until you come to him.' And so a fourth motif is added to the other three: that of the healing of the Maimed King by Galahad. The motifs are, however, still distributed in groups of three: the first group contains the miraculous weapon, the wound inflicted upon a king, and the devastation of the land, but *not* the miraculous healing; the second omits the devastation of the land, but adds the healing, no doubt as a means of stressing Galahad's super-natural powers.

These same patterns reappear in a branch of the Cycle written after the *Queste del Saint Graal*, the *Estoire del Graal*, which, apart from some additional details, provides exact parallels to the two

implication seems to be that the land was laid waste by the sword which caused the knight's death.

[1] On the date of the *Queste* see *Romania*, lvii. 137–46 (F. Lot) and J. Frappier, *Étude sur la Mort le roi Artu* (Paris, 1936), 133–8. The latest possible date seems to be between 1225 and 1230, but the *terminus a quo* might well be some fifteen years earlier.

[2] *La Queste del Saint Graal*, ed. Albert Pauphilet (Classiques français du moyen âge (Paris, 1923)), 204: 'Si en avint si grant pestilence et si grant persecucion es deus roiaumes que onques puis les terres ne rendirent as laboureors lor travaus, car puis n'i crut ne blé ne autre chose, ne li arbre ne porterent fruit, ne en l'eve ne furent trové poisson, se petit non. Et por ce a len apelee la terre des deus roiaumes la Terre Gaste, por ce que par cel dolereus cop avoit esté agastie.' The 'dolereus cop' was aimed at King Lambar, a 'pious man', by his defeated enemy King Varlan who, in despair of finding a weapon with which to defend himself against Lambar, seized a miraculous sword and struck him with it; but no sooner did he put it back into the scabbard than he himself dropped dead.

[3] The king, whose name is variously spelt in the manuscripts (Parlan, Pelles, Pellinor, etc.), having lost his way in the forest while hunting with his knights, comes to the sea shore, sees a ship, and going on board finds a sword; but as he draws it from the scabbard he is struck by a lance *par mi oultre les deus cuisses* so grievously that he remains maimed for many years. Cf. *La Queste*, ed. Pauphilet, p. 209.

incidents in the *Queste*;[1] and it is not until we come to a work
which is later than the Cycle proper that a single pattern containing
the four motifs begins to emerge. This work is an adaptation or, as
some would call it, a continuation of the Cycle; it has no title, but
it is sometimes described by the totally inappropriate name of
La Suite du Merlin.[2] One section of it is known to English readers
through Malory and Tennyson as the *Romance of Balin*, the Knight
with the Two Swords, and it is in this section that our four themes
are at last combined into a single story. Balin, the 'unhappy knight',
le chevalier mescheant, is pursued by misfortune. He is the embodiment of the dark powers beating against Arthurian knighthood,
of the 'hunger', to use Charles Williams's phrase, 'with which
creation preys upon itself'. A strange fatality dogs his steps where-
ever he goes, and whoever travels under his protection is struck
dead by an invisible hand. At last Balin discovers the name of the
murderer: it is Garlan, the brother of King Pelleam (or Pellehem).
In spite of Merlin's warning Balin is determined to seek revenge.
He goes to the castle where King Pelleam holds court, sits down
with other knights in the castle hall, but refuses to partake of the
meal. Garlan, the 'red-haired knight', takes this as an insult and
strikes Balin in the face, whereupon Balin draws his sword and
kills him. King Pelleam challenges Balin, and in the ensuing combat
Balin's sword is broken. He rushes through the castle looking for

[1] Cf. *The Vulgate Version of the Arthurian Romances*, ed. H. Oskar Sommer, vol. i
(Washington, 1909), 80–1, 290. In the first of these passages the angel, having
wounded Josephé, explains that no one will be wounded by the lance except one man:
'Cil sera rois et descendra de ton lignage . . . Cil en sera ferus par mi les cuisses, ne
ja ne garira jusques a tant que les merveilles dou Graal seront descouvertes a celui
qui sera pleins de toutez bontez' (Brit. Mus. MS. Royal 19 C. XII, f. 22c). The second
passage specifies: 'devant ce que Galaad le trés bon chevalier le vendra visiter'.

[2] Such evidence as we have suggests that this work was written between 1230
and 1235: it is later than the 'Vulgate' Cycle and earlier than the *Palamède* (cf. E. G.
Gardner, *The Arthurian Legend in Italian Literature* (London, 1930), pp. 205–6). On
the place of the *Suite* in Arthurian Literature see Dr. Fanni Bogdanow's chapter in
Arthurian Literature in the Middle Ages, ed. R. S. Loomis (Oxford, 1959); on its textual
history cf. my *Genèse de la Suite du Merlin* in *Mélanges de philologie romane et de littérature
médiévale offerts à Ernest Hoepffner* (Paris, 1949), 295–300. The only French text containing a complete account of the Waste Land episode is MS. Add. 7071 of the
Cambridge University Library which first came to light in 1945. There are two
editions of the relevant portion of the *Suite* based on MS. Add. 38117 of the British
Museum (formerly known as the 'Huth Merlin'): *Merlin*, ed. G. Paris and J. Ulrich
(Paris, 1886), i. 212–ii. 60, and *Le Roman de Balain*, ed. M. D. Legge (Manchester,
1942).

another weapon until he sees the open door of a large room. Once inside he hears a voice saying: '*Mar i entres, car tu n'es mie dignes d'entrer en si haut lieu.*'[1] Ignoring the warning, he seizes a weapon, a lance which stands upright upon a silver table, and with it strikes the king. The castle crashes to the earth and Balin lies unconscious among its ruins for three days and three nights until Merlin comes to deliver him. The king is grievously wounded, and as Balin rides through the country he finds the trees withered and the crops destroyed, and everything laid waste as though lightning had struck the entire land. Everywhere he sees people lying dead; knights and townsfolk in the cities and labourers in the fields. And so this kingdom came to be called the Kingdom of the Blighted Land. As for King Pelleam, he lay where he had been struck and would never have recovered but for Galahad who healed him with the Holy Grail, the vessel brought to England by Joseph of Arimathea. King Pelleam was, as Malory has it in his adaptation of the Balin story, 'nigh of Joseph's kin, and that was the most worshipfullest man alive in those days, and great pity it was of his hurt, for through that stroke it turned to great dole, tray and teen'.[2]

In a late version of the Grail quest preserved in a single manuscript,[3] the description of the healing of the Maimed King by Galahad contains a significant reference to Balin. The Maimed King says to Galahad: 'Look at the dolorous wound which I received from the Knight with the two Swords. Through this wound many misfortunes have befallen.'[4] Here, then, at long last the Sword,

---

[1] 'In an evil hour have you come here, for you are not worthy to enter such a holy place' (MS. Cambridge Add. 7071, f. 270, col. 2). The context is as follows: 'Il entent bien la voice, mais pur ceo ne laisse il pas sa voie, ainz se fiert en la chamber et troeve que ele est si bele et si riche qu'il ne quidast mie qu'en toute le monde eust sa paraille de biauté. La chamber estoit quarré et grans a mervaille, et soef flerant ainsi come se toutez lez espicez du monde i fussent apporteez. En mi lieu de la chamber avoit un tabel d'argent mult grante [et] haute par raison, et seoit sor trois pilerez d'argent; et desus la tabel, droit en mi lieu, avoit un orçuel d'argent et d'or, et dedenz cele orçuel estoit une lance drescie la point desoz et le haut desuz.'

[2] Cf. *The Works of Sir Thomas Malory* (Oxford, 1967), 85, 1315–17.

[3] MS. B.N. fr. 343.

[4] 'Veez ci li doloreux cop que li Chevaliers as Deus Espees fist. Par cestui cop sunt maint mal avenu; ce me poise' (MS. B.N. fr. 343, f. 103a). The text was published by Dr. Fanni Bogdanow in her *Romance of the Grail* (p. 254). The passage describing the healing reads as follows: 'Et les plaies estoient encor ausint fresches com li jor memes qu'il avoit esté feruz. Et Galahaz adente le vessel ou il cuidoit bien qu'il n'eust riens, et au verser qu'il fist il vit cheoir sor les plaies trois goutes de sanc.'

the Maimed King, the Waste Land, and the miraculous healing
are brought together. The chronology of our texts shows that
this was achieved by a writer who had before him the material
gathered by others, but who set himself the task of arranging
and elaborating it; a writer, moreover, who performed this task
so successfully that the four motifs which for a long time had
existed in various combinations of two or three now became
inseparable from one another. Needless to say, if the chronology
could be ignored there would be room not only for Jessie Weston's
attempt to project the story 'as a whole' into a mythological or
ritual past, but for a variety of other theories. In his learned and
abundantly documented *Légende arthurienne et le Graal* M. Jean
Marx builds up a pre-literary Celtic pattern (*schème*) of the legend
on the basis of the Grail romances, but to do this he has to arrange
these in reverse chronological order. The *Suite du Merlin*[1] comes
first, then the 'First Continuation' of Chrétien's *Conte del Graal*,[2]
and lastly the French source of Wolfram von Eschenbach's *Parzival*,[3]
that is to say either Chrétien's poem or its model, if there ever was
one. This arrangement makes it possible to trace the Balin story
to an imaginary pattern quite unlike any of the early texts we
possess. It is tempting to speculate on the kind of pattern critics
might one day propose as a substitute for the Greek legend of
Hippolytus if they achieve the same degree of freedom from
chronology in dealing with Euripides' *Hippolytus*, Seneca's *Phaedra*,
and Racine's *Phèdre*; for it is not simply a matter of ignoring the
existing chronology, but of *replacing it by another*. When A. C. L.
Brown discovered that the story of Balin was, as he put it, 'in the
whole range of Arthurian romance the most coherent and detailed
explanation of the machinery of the Grail Quest',[4] he immediately
concluded that it must represent the Celtic original from which
all the other versions of the Grail Quest and of the Waste Land
theme were evolved. To him as to Jean Marx, Jessie Weston, and
their many followers, anything that was structurally complete
must *ipso facto* represent an early state of the tradition. The philo-

[1] p. 258.   [2] p. 259.   [3] pp. 260-1.
[4] 'The Bleeding Lance', *Publications of the Modern Language Association of America*,
xxv (1910), N.S. xviii. 50.

sophy behind this assumption is not unlike that of the man who, when asked to say what he thought about a particularly bad piece of verse, replied that 'somebody must have written it himself'. Any good piece of verse must of necessity be the work of 'someone else'. On this view the various versions of the Waste Land story can only be placed in the order of diminishing coherence, quite regardless of the fact that this happens to be also the reverse chronological order; and an elaborate mythological or traditional background has to be conjured up in order to account for the appearance of the best among them which is presumed to be the earliest. The mythology, or the hypothetical pre-literary tradition, may have an attraction all its own, but it seems at best unreasonable to accept it as a substitute for the one solid reality that we possess—the texts as we have them and the creative impulse which caused them to develop as they did.

Not that the outcome of their development is always free from imperfections; but the flaws which it conceals are as revealing as any positive achievement. One such flaw in the Balin story is of particular significance. Balin is known as the Knight with the Two Swords: in addition to his own sword he carries the one which he took against her will from a damsel who had been sent to Arthur's court by *la dame de l'isle Avalon*.[1] The damsel told him that the sword would bring disaster, and the prophecy was fulfilled, for it was with this same sword that Balin killed in single combat his own brother Balan, whom he had failed to recognize. At the time of the combat with King Pelleam he had the two swords with him, and it is not clear why, when one of them broke, he did not use the other instead of rushing as he did from one room of the castle to another in the hope of finding a weapon with which to defend himself.[2] The faulty motivation suggests that the story

[1] The damsel first asks King Arthur to find a knight who could untie the thong surrounding the sword and take the sword out of its scabbard. After Arthur and many of his knights have failed in the attempt, Balin 'met les mains as neus et les desnoue erraument et tire l'espee a lui' (*Le Roman de Balain*, ed. M. D. Legge, p. 7). But he refuses to give the sword back to the damsel and she warns him that it will bring misfortune: 'Car bien sachiés que li hom que vous primes en ochirrés, sera li hom ou monde que vous plus amés' (ibid., p. 8).

[2] The two adapters of the French romance, Malory and the author of the Spanish *Demanda del Sancto Grial*, solved the problem each in his own way. Malory simply says

was a combination of originally independent themes which did not completely fit together. It might have been better to have chosen as the protagonist a knight who did not carry more than one sword; but Balin was *li chevaliers mescheans*, the most unhappy knight in the world who brought ill luck wherever he went. Misfortune came his way in an unusual fashion: instead of being defeated in combat he was forced to inflict miseries on other people as no knight had ever done before. Challenged by an Irish knight he kills him; although by all standards of chivalric behaviour his action is fully justified, he can only lament it, and his regret turns to despair when a damsel comes to mourn the death of the victim and stabs herself with the dead knight's sword. On another occasion Balin meets a knight who is anxiously awaiting his beloved and they set out together to find her. Once more, for all his good intentions, he brings disaster: with his help the lady is found, but she is found in the arms of another man. This, Balin thinks, will cure his friend of his unhappy love by showing him what folly it is to put one's heart in a woman's hands. But the knight bitterly reproaches Balin for having brought him to the scene; in anger he draws his sword and kills the two lovers. He has a momentary sense of relief as if stunned by his own stroke; but when he sees what he has done he utters a cry of despair and stabs himself with the same sword. And so Balin's finest deeds turn to disaster. In his endeavour to serve his fellow men he destroys their happiness, not because he is a guilty man who deserves punishment, but because fatality pursues its course and turns his noblest thoughts into crimes. This is precisely what makes him the ideal protagonist of the Waste Land theme. He is the exact converse of Galahad, the long-awaited bearer of a sacred mission who comes to Arthur's court to break an evil spell. On Galahad's first appearance at Camelot Arthur says to him: 'We

that when Balin's sword broke he was 'wepynles' and 'ran into a chambir for to seke a wepyn' (*The Works of Sir Thomas Malory*, p. 84). How Balin recovered the weapon with which he was to kill his brother (pp. 89–91) Malory does not say. The Spanish adapter is more subtle. He says that Balin had left the sword he had received from 'la donzella' in a sort of ante-room from which he eventually retrieved it (ed. Adolfo Bonilla y San Martín (Madrid 1907), 109, 111). The explanation is clearly an after-thought on the Spanish author's part. In the scene of Balin's arrival in King Pelleam's castle all the extant versions are in complete agreement with one another.

had great need of your coming for many reasons, for there are in this land many great marvels to be achieved which no one else can bring to an end.' Galahad achieves all these marvels. He delivers the captives from the Castle of Maidens, changes the course of a battle at a tournament which symbolizes the struggle between good and evil, and is hailed as the deliverer by King Pelleam, the Maimed King, who knows that he can now die in peace. The advent of Balin the 'unhappy knight' was to serve as a prelude to this liberation: it was to darken the scene which Galahad was to illumine by his mere presence; it was to cast a spell which Galahad alone could break. None other than Balin could have performed this task more naturally; none, by the mere fact of being what he was, could have afflicted the kingdom of Logres with the evils which Galahad was to cure. The *non sequitur* resulting from the fact that he was also the 'Knight with the Two Swords' makes it clear that the story developed by stages; that what we have before us is not an organic pattern originally conceived as a whole, but a product of an ingenious 'assembling' of the existing elements in a new sequence.[1]

At its best, the method can be compared to the action of a magnet placed under a piece of glass, the upper surface of which has been sprinkled with iron filings: each filing would then assume a particular direction and the entire mass would map out the lines of force operating in the magnetic field, forming regular patterns in accordance with the natural law which governs their disposition. Exceptions may occur; just as a filing may escape the impact of the magnet, an episode may not find its proper motivation; but, despite such accidents, the all-pervading influence, of which the power of the magnet is the obvious symbol, will go on increasing in strength and will produce in the end all the great cyclic compositions of the thirteenth, fourteenth, and fifteenth centuries. I can hardly hope to show in the remaining few chapters all that this magnetic power brought forth during that period of the history of romance. The Waste Land theme itself follows, of course, the

---

[1] On a parallel development in medieval architecture see Fr. Amada von Scheltema, 'Formkonjunktionen in der Kunstgeschichte', in *Studium Generale*, iii (1950), 698–700, and Zygmunt Swiechowski, 'La formation de l'œuvre architecturale au cours du haut moyen âge', in *Cahiers de civilisation médiévale* (Poitiers, July–Sept. 1958), 377–8.

familiar 'sequential' pattern: its four component parts, once put
together, succeed each other in a causal sequence—the Sword,
the Stroke, the blighted land, and the blight removed by the
healing of the victim's wound. But in none of the works that have
come down to us does this sequence exist on its own. It is invariably
part of a much more elaborate design—one of a number of threads
in a vast woven fabric. Each of these threads is caught in a movement which reflects the deeper aspirations of narrative form, its
final and triumphant flowering. A complex network of themes
stretches over the richly decorated volumes in which Arthurian
romances have come down to us. Seeing these vast compositions from
outside, puzzled by their inordinate size and complexity, a casual
observer may not perceive the subtle logic of their growth. He
may fail to notice that they conceal a structure more complete
and coherent than any that has been seen before. And if he happens
to find traces of such a structure, he is likely to regard it not as
the work of the romance writers themselves, but as a spontaneous
product of popular fancy, miraculously preserved and almost
untouched by those who transmitted it to us. Poets will build their
dreams upon such visions and men of learning will be guided by
them in their attempt to reconstruct whatever lies behind the
evidence of the written word.

But as the mirage melts into thin air there comes inevitably
into our field of consciousness an achievement beside which
speculations about pre-literary traditions will seem a vain pursuit,
and the myth of the deterioration of poetic values a strange
delusion. There is a curious echo of this myth in Goethe's *Werther*.
Werther says, no doubt rightly, that in telling stories to children
one must never change what has once been said, because for a
child to change a story is to spoil it. But he goes on to say that
'human nature can be made to believe the strangest things which,
once accepted, cling fast, and woe betide the man who tries to
blot them out'. He forgets that art, 'playing second Nature's part',
can supply whatever Nature has omitted. Spenser knew this, and
so did Valéry when he asserted that genius was *not* the immediate
impulse which brought forth, before anyone else had thought of
it, the one and only thing that mattered: genius, as Valéry has it,

is the power 'to grasp the value of what has already been found'—
'la promptitude à comprendre la valeur de ce qui vient de se
produire et à saisir ce produit'.[1] Invention, according to this view,
presupposes two actions, or even two agents: one gathers things
together, the other discovers their latent energy and value.[2]
Valéry was, of course, thinking primarily of what takes place
within a single mind; but the same process can operate between
two or several minds separated in time and space, for the definition
of the function of genius remains valid no matter how long and
laborious the preparation: significance, as some of the most
clear-sighted philosophers have told us, is essentially an adventitious value. And once this essential fact is grasped, the traditional trend of medieval literary studies can be reversed, the
flight into the realm of legend arrested: literary history, instead
of retrogressing, as it generally does, towards the dark uncertain-
ties of Valéry's 'first man', can then begin to follow the light
which illumines the path of the second—the steep and adventurous
path of creation.

[1] *Tel Quel*, ii. 234.
[2] Ibid.: 'l'autre choisit, reconnaît ce qu'il désire et ce qui lui importe dans
l'ensemble des produits du premier'.

V

THE POETRY OF INTERLACE

To apply intelligence to the matter in hand, to go in search of stories waiting to be redeemed, to elucidate them, such was, I believe, the task undertaken by French romance writers in the twelfth century, and the flowering of the genre in later years was a measure of their success. When Chrétien de Troyes proudly contrasted his achievement as a narrator with the unskilled, rambling efforts of story-tellers who did not know how to construct a narrative out of 'tales of adventure', he made it clear that the purpose of poetic composition as he saw it was to give meaning and coherence to amorphous matter. His most subtle and most effective method was an analysis—sometimes simply an explanation—of the characters' motives and feelings. The narrative proper might remain simple and even bare; what mattered was its systematic and careful elucidation. Thirteenth-century prose writers, and especially those who took it upon themselves to exploit and to expand the rich legacy of Arthurian romance, had the same ultimate purpose in mind: they too wanted to make the narrative more meaningful by giving it a 'causal' perspective; but the method they adopted was a typically thirteenth-century one, paralleled in several other aspects of late medieval thought and imagination. It consisted less in explaining the action in so many words than in forging significant and tangible links between originally independent episodes; it aimed at establishing, or at least suggesting, relationships between hitherto unrelated themes; it illustrated, better perhaps than any other contemporary form of art could have done, the scholastic principle of *manifestatio*.[1]

As we examine the growth of Arthurian romance we see this principle at work everywhere and at all levels. But the irony of it is that as we reach the summit of its development, far from

[1] Cf. Erwin Panofsky, *Gothic Architecture and Scholasticism* (Cleveland and New York, 1957). See esp. pp. 27–60.

being enlightened, we tend to feel confused. Arthurian romance in its most advanced cyclic form[1] becomes a work so complex as to defeat at first every attempt to discover any semblance of rational principle behind it. The knights-errant who indefatigably make their way through a forest—that ancient symbol of uncertain fate—are apt to abandon at any time one quest for the sake of another, only to be sidetracked again a moment later; and when such things happen they behave as though their apparent vagaries were part of an accepted mode of living, requiring no apology or explanation. They speak as though they were involved, not, as we would imagine, in a series of unhappy accidents, but in an enviable pursuit, to be sought after and enjoyed. The most clear-sighted among the nineteenth-century critics naturally failed to make sense of the resulting maze of adventures, quests, and battles: Gaston Paris admitted that there were in the late romances of chivalry examples of fine prose,[2] but found the narrative 'incoherent', 'obscure', 'hollow', and even 'absurd'.[3] Other scholars followed suit and it soon became a commonplace of criticism to speak of these romances as an unfortunate accident of literary history, to condemn and deplore their uninspired prolixity. Gustav Gröber, among others, unable as he was to find in them anything resembling a 'central theme' ('Grundgedanke'), thought that there was nothing there except an accumulation of stories 'without shape

[1] In its complete form the 'Vulgate' contains five branches: *L'Estoire del Graal*, *L'Estoire de Merlin*, the *Lancelot* proper, *La Queste del Saint Graal*, and *La Mort le Roi Artu*, the last three forming the complete *'prose Lancelot'* or *Lancelot du Lac*. The Cycle appeared in all probability between 1220 and 1225, though the *terminus a quo* may be pushed back as far as 1215, and was followed by *Tristan de Léonois*, a voluminous prose version of the Tristan story largely inspired by the 'Vulgate'. The *Suite du Merlin* (see above, p. 60, n. 2) and the *Roman du Graal* of which it forms part, were written soon after. *Le Roman de Palamède*, closely related to the *Tristan de Léonois*, is slightly later than the *Suite*, but was in existence by 1240. Altogether the production of the entire series of Arthurian prose romances took less than a quarter of a century, probably only twenty years.

[2] *La Littérature française au moyen âge* (Paris, 1888, 5th ed. (1914)), 111: 'Pour nous, tant comme conception que comme style, ces romans ont quelque chose de trop factice et de trop maniéré pour nous plaire; mais on ne peut disconvenir qu'ils contiennent de beaux morceaux (notamment le *Tristan*), et qu'ils nous montrent une prose déjà très sûre d'elle-même et s'efforçant de produire des effets artistiques.'

[3] Cf. his remarks in his introduction to *Merlin* (Société des Anciens Textes Français, 1886), pp. xlviii ('l'invraisemblance y est poussée jusqu'à l'absurde, sans réussir à piquer la curiosite') and lxix ('les aventures nous fatiguent par leur creuse et monotone invraisemblance').

or substance'.[1] Both he and Gaston Paris belonged to the generation
of scholars who had set themselves the task of rehabilitating the
literature of medieval Europe; but 'rehabilitation' as they understood it was, as it still is to most people, a matter of finding in
a forgotten text something resembling their own artistic ideal,
and nothing could have been more remote from that ideal than
the romances and the tradition to which they belonged. For all
the changes of taste and fashion that occurred between the end of
the sixteenth century and the end of the nineteenth, the concept
of poetic perfection had remained fundamentally the same, and
Montaigne's reaction to medieval writings had lost none of its
significance in the intervening three hundred years. It was
Montaigne who wrote in his first book of essays—I quote from
Florio's not very accurate translation: 'Of King Arthur, of Lancelot
du Lake, of Amadis, of Huon de Bordeaux and such idle time-
consuming and wit-besotting trash of books, wherein youth does
commonly amuse itself, I was not so much as acquainted with
their names, and to this day know not of their bodies nor what
they contain: so exact was my discipline.'[2]

To account for the paradox of clarification resulting in what
some would regard as greater obscurity, we must bear in mind
that clarity and simplicity are different concepts and that simple
things are not necessarily more intelligible than complex ones.
Our failure to realize this stems from the traditional belief that
simplicity is a virtue and complexity a fault[3]—from the convention

---

[1] *Grundriß der romanischen Philologie*, ii. 726: 'Die Erzählweise dieser Prosadich-
tungen . . . geht, wie die der Fortsetzer Chrestiens im *Graal*, auf Häufung aus. Der
Grundgedanke wird Nebensache, die Episode drängt sich vor, über dem Retardieren
wird kein Ende erreicht und der Ziel verfehlt.'

[2] Montaigne does not mention King Arthur and uses fewer derogatory epithets:
'Des *Lancelot du Lac*, des *Amadis*, des *Huon de Bordeaux*, et tel fatras de livres à quoy
l'enfance s'amuse, je n'en connoissois pas seulement le nom, ny ne fais encore le corps
[= 'the matter'], tant exacte estoit ma discipline' (*Essais*: 'De l'institution des enfants',
Œuvres complètes, ed. Albert Thibaudet and Maurice Rat (Paris, 1965), 175. Cf. also
p. 389). Over half a century later Chapelain spoke of the romances in even more violent terms: 'L'auteur est barbare, qui a écrit durant la barbarie et pour des barbares
seulement; il ne s'est jamais douté de ce que c'était qu'un plan d'ouvrage, qu'une
disposition légitime, qu'un plus juste rapport des parties, qu'un nœud subtil ni qu'un
dénouement.'

[3] According to Hurd, 'the supreme art of the designer' and 'the truest taste in
gardening' consist 'in disposing his ground and objects into an *entire landskip*; and
grouping them . . . in so easy a manner that the careless observer, tho' he be taken

which requires any 'good' piece of writing to be structurally
transparent and to develop, as it were, along a straight line with
a minimum of deviation. The vast forest in which knights-errant
seek adventures is a visual expression of everything that this
convention condemns: it is the exact opposite of the Aristotelian
idea of a work to be 'embraced in a single view'.[1] In the words of
C. S. Lewis, it is 'something that cannot be taken in at a glance
something that at first looks planless, though all is planned'.[2]
The modern literary historian, with his limited range of aesthetic
notions and his correspondingly limited critical vocabulary,[3]
is quite unable to describe, let alone explain, this type of structure
except as an unfortunate departure from a recognized norm. It
is therefore all the more significant that the first modern scholar
to suggest a new approach to the thirteenth-century romances
of chivalry was neither a literary critic nor a historian of literature,
but a historian of medieval institutions, Ferdinand Lot.[4] In an
endeavour to prove that the major part of the 'Lancelot-Grail'
Cycle was the work of one man (a point which he failed to establish),
Lot made the all-important discovery that no single section of the
Cycle is self-contained: earlier or later adventures are recalled or
announced, as the case may be, in any given part of the work.
To achieve this the author, or authors, had recourse to a narrative
device known to earlier writers, including Ovid, but never before
used on so vast a scale, namely the device of interweaving a number
of separate themes. Far from being a mosaic from which any one

with the symmetry of the whole, discovers no art in the combination' (*Letters on
Chivalry and Romance*, ed. Edith J. Morley (London, 1911), 122–3). In support of these
remarks Hurd quotes Tasso's famous lines:

> E quel, che'l bello, e'l caro accresce à l'opere,
> L'Arte, che tutto fà, nulla si scopre.

[1] To be 'easily embraced in a single view' or 'easily taken in by the mind'
(εὐσύνοπτος) is, according to Aristotle (*Poetics*, ch. xxiii), one of the features of a
properly unified composition.
[2] *The Discarded Image*, p. 194. In the following pages I have reproduced in an
expanded form parts of my essay on *Form and Meaning in Medieval Romance* (Cambridge,
1966), Presidential Address of the Modern Humanities Research Association.
[3] These strictures do not apply to modern *critics* who have greatly extended our
horizon, but who seldom concern themselves with medieval texts.
[4] In his study of the prose *Lancelot* published in 1918 under the title of *Étude sur
le Lancelot en prose*. See esp. the chapter entitled 'Le principe de l'entrelacement'
(pp. 17 ff.).

stone could be removed without upsetting the rest, the Cycle turned out to be remarkably like the fabric of matting or tapestry; a single cut across it, made at any point, would unravel it all.[1] And yet it was clearly not a unified body of material: it consisted of a variety of themes, all distinct and yet inseparable from one another. 'Everything leads to everything else, but by very intricate paths. At every point the question "How did we get here?" arises, but there is always an answer.'[2]

What could be more puzzling, not to say alarming? How could a structure consisting of a large number of themes without a common beginning, middle, and end, in other words a narrative devoid of *unity* in our sense of the term, be as impregnable as a composition revolving round a single centre and constructed like a well-made play? Had we not learnt from Aristotle that such a thing could never happen? That unless the golden rule about the beginning, the middle, and the end was observed, no work of art could have any proper solidity? Surely, if the rule were ignored altogether, any part of the work could be removed without damaging the whole. How, then, could one account for an eminently *acentric* composition, with as much internal cohesion as one would find in any centralized pattern?

Ferdinand Lot, concerned as he was exclusively with the problem of authorship, never stopped to consider any of these questions. He was like the man who went to look for silver and found gold, not realizing what it was that he had found. Some thirty-five years later, and quite independently of Lot, C. S. Lewis writing about Spenser and looking further into the history of the interwoven narrative—which he called *polyphonic*—realized that this was the very thing that had dominated the European literary scene for centuries.

When we know [he wrote] that civilized audiences in so many different countries went on demanding it, and that Tasso's father (also a poet) lost all his popularity when he wrote a narrative poem without it, common sense will surely make us pause before we assume that it was simply wrong and that the technique of modern fiction is simply

---

[1] Lot, p. 28: 'Si l'on tente d'y pratiquer une coupure, tout part en morceaux.'
[2] C. S. Lewis, loc. cit.

right. The old polyphonic story, after all, enjoyed a longer success than the modern novel has enjoyed yet. We do not know which will seem the more considerable literary phenomenon to a critic looking back from the year 2500. Such reflections [C. S. Lewis concluded] should induce us to give the old technique, at least, a fair trial.[1]

But the fact remains that even if we are only going to give it a 'fair trial', we must first silence certain aesthetic reactions which have become second nature to us. We can come to terms with most Renaissance writers because, although they may occasionally be in sympathy with the medieval technique, they are aware of other principles of composition. When Tasso says that 'natural multiplicity' in a narrative adds to its artistic perfection because it brings the work closer to Nature,[2] we may agree or disagree with him, but we can follow his argument; and the reason why we can follow it is that for Tasso, as for his contemporaries, something resembling our concept of unity exists, even though they may qualify or even reject it. What is difficult for us to grasp is the attitude of people whose minds had never been conditioned by this concept, and a literary theory which is alien to all that this concept implies.

One of the best formulations of the Aristotelian notion of unity is that proposed by Giovambattista Strozzi: 'Indivisible in itself, but divided from other things.'[3] Few medieval epics and romances would fit this definition; and it is doubtful whether the implied conception of unity as something which cuts the work off from any other matter would have appealed to any writer of consequence in the last centuries of the Middle Ages. To Saint Bonaventura order and perfection were synonymous with the elaboration of

---

[1] *Major British Writers*, under the general editorship of G. B. Harrison (New York, 1954), i. 97–8 (introduction to extracts from Spenser by C. S. Lewis).

[2] *Discorso delle differenze poetiche per risposta al Signor Orazio Ariosto* (Prose scelte (Milan, 1925), first published in 1587), 115–16: 'Nè minor riguardo dobbiamo avere negli episodj; perchè, quantunque gli episodj si possano frapporre nella favola versimilmente, nondimeno è viziosa quella favola nella quale gli episodj sono in altro modo inseriti, e si chiama favola episodica: ma l'arte allora è più perfetta, ch'ella più s'assimiglia alla natura.' On Tasso's conception of unity see Bernard Weinberg, *A History of Literary Criticism in the Italian Renaissance* (Chicago, 1961), 1055–8.

[3] *Dell'unità della favola* (written in 1599, published in 1635): 'indivisibile in sè, e divisa dell'altre'. Cf. Weinberg, op. cit., p. 149.

the material, with its multiplication and its development,[1] whereas
to us terms such as 'order' and 'perfection' naturally suggest a
process of selection and simplification.[2]

A significant instance of an open conflict between these two
approaches to the art of narrative occurs in the writings of the
Italian Renaissance as part of the Ariosto–Tasso controversy. The
partisans of Ariosto champion the cause of 'multiplicity', the
partisans of Tasso that of unity. The former have no hesitation
in saying that unity is apt to impoverish a work of art by 'elimi-
nating episode, ornament and substance'.[3] In saying this they rely
quite as much on their reading of late medieval fiction as on
certain features of medieval rhetoric. For one of the things that
distinguish medieval treatises on the art of poetry from their
Roman models is precisely the treatment of amplification. The
classical doctrine of *amplificatio* or αὔξησις was concerned with the
art of making small things great, of 'raising acts and personal
traits above their dimensions'. It was based upon the demand,
originally made by Gorgias and later by Isocrates and Aristotle,
that the orator should know how to present great things as if

[1] 'Si esset unitas non esset pulchritudo, quia non esset ordo et perfectio', *Itiner-
arium*, ii, 40. Cf. Edgar de Bruyne, *Études d'esthétique médiévale* (Bruyge, 1946), iii. 216.
[2] The distinction between unity of theme and cohesion of themes—fundamental
to medieval literary aesthetics—has not so far been sufficiently clearly brought out
by historians of medieval thought. It is entirely absent from the relevant section of
M. Edgar de Bruyne's *Esthétique du moyen âge* (Louvain, 1947), 250–1. He writes:
'La loi esthétique fondamentale est, aux yeux du moyen âge, l'unité dans la variété.
Nous savons que cette variété accompagne une multiplicité surabondante qui dans les
arts, par exemple dans la cathédrale, dans la chanson de geste, dans le mystère, ne fait
que reproduire l'innombrable variété de l'univers physique. Mais quel que soit le sentiment moderne au sujet de l'unité artistique, l'historien ne peut nier que les esthéti-
ciens médiévaux en avaient une conscience vive. La qualité principale de l'œuvre
littéraire est, pour eux, la cohérence.' It is difficult to credit *all* forms of medieval
literature with 'cohérence', and even more difficult to identify the latter with 'unité'.
[3] Lionardo Salviati (*Degli Accademici della Crusca difesa dell' Orlando Furioso dell'*,
Ariosto, etc. (Florence, 1584). p. 16ᵛ) maintains that multiplicity as used by Ariosto
is a positive merit: 'la tela, e non le fila è quella, che deę essere una nell' Epopeia:
e tale è quella del Furioso: me tela larga, e magnifica, e ripiena di molte fila' (quoted
by Bernard Weinberg, op. cit., p. 1007). Giraldi Cintio (*Discorsi*, 1554) and Malatesta (*Della poesia romanzesca*, 1596) express similar views. As Weinberg aptly puts it,
'what critics of Ariosto had singled out as a defect in his work is here (i.e. in Cintio's
Discorsi) transformed into an expedient for achieving interest, sympathy and suspense. The principle of organization comes to be referred to a broader principle,
useful for all aspects of Ariosto's work, that of variety. Variety, not unity, is the
fundamental criterion' (op. cit., p. 969).

they were small and small things as if they were great. The
medieval variety of amplification was a horizontal rather than
a vertical extension—an expansion or an unrolling of a number of
interlocked themes.[1] Hence the insistence on *digressio* as a device
of special importance, recommended by Martianus Capella,[2]
praised for its elegance by Cassiodorus,[3] and eloquently advocated
by Geoffrey of Vinsauf and John Garland.[4] Geoffrey suggests
two methods of using it: to digress into another part of the matter
('ad aliam partem materiae') or to introduce another matter
('aliquid extra materiam'). In the former case digression would
serve either as a reminder or as an anticipation of something that
belongs to the matter in hand; in the latter, it would amount to a
diversion, a change of theme, but with the implied assurance that
the narration would eventually be resumed at the point at which
it was interrupted:

> Deinde revertor
> Unde prius digressus sum.[5]

John Garland, a pupil of Alain de Lille and himself one of the
'curriculum authors', while differing in some respects from
Geoffrey,[6] also looked upon digression as a particularly elegant
variety of *amplificatio*, and, like everybody else of his time, treated
the latter not as an upward movement but as a linear expansion.

Carried to its logical conclusion, this doctrine would not only
justify but call for the very things that our conventional poetics
condemn outright. It would call not for monocentric unity but
for expansion and diversity, for growth, both real and hypothetical: real when a theme or a sequence of themes is lengthened

---

[1] Cf. E. R. Curtius, op cit., p. 485: '*Amplificatio* als *auxesis* ist Erhöhung und gehört
der vertikalen Dimension an, *amplificatio* als *dilatatio* der horizontalen.' The normal
form of *amplificatio* in medieval rhetoric is that which is synonymous with *dilatatio*.
On the possible classical parallels to this doctrine see Hennig Brinkmann, *Wesen
und Form der mittelalterischen Dichtung* (Halle, 1928), 47–50, and Curtius, op cit.,
pp. 485–6.

[2] Ed. Dick, 175. 8.

[3] Cf. H. Nickstadt, *De digressionibus quibus in Variis usus est Cassiodorus* (Marburg,
1921).

[4] *Documentum de modo et arte versificandi*, ii. 2. 17, ed. Faral in *Arts poétiques du XII*^e
et du XIIIe *siècles* (Paris, 1924), 274. Cf. also p. 74.

[5] *Poetria Nova*, 536. 5, ed. Faral, op. cit., p. 236.

[6] Cf. *Poetria*, ed. G. Mari (*Romanische Forschungen XIII*), 193.

within an existing work; hypothetical when the author projects a possible continuation into the future, to be carried out by a successor who in turn will bequeath a similar projection to those who will follow him.

And because, as C. S. Lewis puts it, 'the (improbable) adventure which we are following is liable at any moment to be interrupted by some quite different (improbable) adventures, there steals upon us unawares the conviction that adventures of this sort are going on all round us, that in this vast forest (we are nearly always in a forest) this is the sort of thing that goes on all the time, that it was going on before we arrived and will continue after we have left'.[1] This is precisely what the authors of the Arthurian Prose Cycle strove to achieve: the feeling that there is no single beginning and no single end, that each initial adventure can be extended into the past and each final adventure into the future by a further lengthening of the narrative threads. Any theme can reappear after an interval so as to stretch the whole fabric still further until the reader loses every sense of limitation in time or space. And any theme is, of course, 'indivisible' *both* within itself and 'from other things': it is not even divisible from themes yet to be developed, from works yet to be written.

The next and possibly the decisive step towards a proper understanding of cyclic romance is the realization that since it is always possible, and often even necessary, for several themes to be pursued simultaneously, they have to alternate like threads in a woven fabric, one theme interrupting another and again another, and yet all remaining constantly present in the author's and the reader's mind. The adventures which constitute the great cycles of romances thus become part of a carefully thought-out design of fantastic dimensions—of a narrative composition in which a coherence of the subtlest kind exists, though it is conveyed, not, as most modern readers would expect, through explanatory observations and discourses, but through the amplification and expansion of the matter itself—a device which it

---

[1] *Major British Writers*, p. 98. How much force there is in C. S. Lewis's suggestion that the method was ultimately derived from Ovid's *Metamorphoses* is another matter. In the case of so general a phenomenon the influence of any particular model, however famous, is not likely to have been a decisive factor.

ve est haine mlt encoche
quele espone mole
z broche ....
dettour amours
quille puet ....
z amort onqs ne semuet

IV. INTERLACE IN THE DESIGN OF A SINGLE COMBAT (Chrétien de Troyes'
Yvain, MS. 125 of the Garrett Collection in Princeton).
By courtesy of Princeton University Library

V. ACANTHUS LEAVES SHAPED AS COILING SPIRALS (Letters of Saint Gregory, MS. B.N. Lat. 2287, f. 2, 11th century)

Photograph Bibliothèque Nationale

will take the modern world nearly half a millennium to rediscover, through the work of a few solitary writers of our own time.

What a challenge all this is, not only to our habitual mode of perception, but to our idea of *possible* modes of perception and, consequently, of composition! 'Organic unity', in the sense in which we commonly use the term, turns out to be a metaphor whose validity is strictly limited in time, and it is our failure to grasp this simple fact that has caused us to overlook the very things that give life and meaning to medieval literary art and to much of our own. The error might have been avoided if more attention had been paid by literary historians to the advances recently made in some of the neighbouring fields. Historians of Romanesque art have shown us, among other things, that the so-called 'ribbon' ornament, which has no beginning, no end, and above all no centre—no 'means of guidance', as one critic puts it—is nevertheless a remarkably *coherent* composition. It contains the same seemingly impossible combination of *acentricity* and *cohesion* as that which characterizes the structure of cyclic romances, and the same excess of constructive subtlety.[1] More than that: the 'morphology' and the 'syntax' of Romanesque motifs have been defined in terms almost directly applicable to the narrative devices of thirteenth-century romance writers; the 'formation of sequences' recalls the formation of 'threads' in a cyclic narrative, and the complex continuity of curves, spirals, and entwined stems corresponds closely to the cyclic interlace. Straightforward progression is abandoned in favour of intertwined patterns, 'the themes run parallel, or entwined, or are brought together as in a chequer of knotting and plaiting'.[2] In a memorable

---

[1] Cf. Jurgis Baltrušaitis, *Stylistique ornementale dans la sculpture romane* (Paris, 1931) —a work the value of which, for the study of medieval aesthetics, can hardly be overestimated. Cf. esp. ch. ii, 'La technique ornementale'.

[2] Wilhelm Worringer, *Form in Gothic*, authorized trans. ed. Herbert Read (London, 1927), 41, 54. Cf. Henri Focillon, *Vie des Formes*, pp. 31–2: 'Au système de la série composée d'éléments discontinus, nettement analysés, fortement rythmés, définissant un espace stable et symétrique qui les protège contre l'imprévu des métamorphoses, fait place le système du labyrinthe, qui procède par synthèses mobiles, dans un espace chatoyant. A l'intérieur du labyrinthe, où la vue chemine sans se reconnaître, rigoureusement égarée par un caprice linéaire qui se dérobe pour rejoindre un but secret, s'élabore une dimension nouvelle qui n'est ni le mouvement ni la profondeur, et qui nous en procure l'illusion.'

passage of his *Vie des formes* Focillon describes how they 'wed their respective curves, meet, fuse and pass into an undulating continuity where the relationship of parts ceases to be self-evident'; and Lamprecht, observing the same examples of multiplication and recurrence in a Romanesque design, remarks that 'the convolutions of patterns seem alternately to seek and to avoid each other, captivating sight and sense in a passionately vital movement'. It is an art which surrenders the 'restful' kind of symmetry for the play of fancy in which both movement and depth are achieved by structural richness and infinite multiplication. 'A continuously increasing activity without pauses or accents is set up, and repetition aims primarily at giving each particular motive a potential infinity.'[1]

To illustrate this properly one would have to spend many long hours looking at Romanesque churches and illuminated manuscripts from the ninth century to the thirteenth: the mere visual enjoyment would be more revealing than the most subtle analysis of the techniques employed by the artists. The plates which accompany these pages are mainly reproductions of ornaments and decorated initials found in eleventh-, twelfth-, and thirteenth-century manuscripts. Two different processes are here at work. One stems from a geometrical design and produces the interlace proper, the other from stylized shapes of living things: plants and animals. The interlace proper consists of threads superimposed upon one another in such a way as to make it impossible to separate them: the onlooker's eye does not normally travel along each thread, but moves either horizontally or vertically—or both—embracing *all* the threads as they come within the field of vision. At whatever point the movement is arrested the area perceived will contain a number of interrupted threads. From the Carolingian period onwards this technique shows increasingly great subtlety and acquires as one of its typical characteristics the 'angular bend'.

[1] Wilhelm Worringer, op. cit., p. 53. Haupt (quoted by Worringer) contrasts the two types of ornament—the 'classical' and the 'northern'—by saying that 'while with its opposed—negative and positive—movement, inwards towards the centre or from the centre outwards, classical ornament terminates within itself, thereby bringing itself to complete rest, northern ornament, beginning at a given point, moves ever further forward in the same direction until it has covered the whole surface, and returns as a natural consequence to itself' (ibid., p. 55).

VI. VARIETIES OF INTERLACE FROM THE SECOND BIBLE OF CHARLES
THE BALD (MS. B.N. Lat. 2, 9th century)

Photograph Bibliothèque Nationale

VII. INTERLACE COMBINED WITH THE UNDULATING
STALK
(The Gradual of Albi, MS. B.N. Lat. 776, 11th century)
Photograph Bibliothèque Nationale

The resulting geometric pattern can be represented thus:—

The non-geometric, or dynamic, pattern is as a rule composed of stalks, leaves, buds, flowers, and fruit of various kinds. To the laurel, olive, ivy, and acanthus leaf inherited from Greek and Roman artists the Middle Ages added vine, clover, thistle, and maple leaf, and freely mixed them with animal heads. The undulating stalk would frequently give rise to designs such as this:—

The flowering curve, stretching as it were beyond the confines of the vegetable kingdom, would sometimes exhibit the head of an animal with its mouth open, ready to swallow a fruit or a flower suspended from another curve.[1]

Ramification of this kind can, from the nature of things, go on indefinitely, but the ultimate matrix of it is the coiling spiral which since ancient times had found its floral counterpart in the ornamental use of the acanthus leaf. Plate V shows one of the most striking examples of this development, reproduced from

[1] These and the following observations will no doubt recall many examples of the same patterns in the ornamental art of other countries and other periods of history. A most impressive account of the similarities between the structure of *Beowulf* and some typical features of Anglo-Saxon ornamental design has recently been given by Professor John Leyerle in his article on 'The Interlace Structure of *Beowulf*' (*University of Toronto Quarterly*, vol. xxxvii, no. 1 (Oct. 1967), 1–17). I have confined myself to illustrations which are geographically and chronologically closest to the literary works with which this study is concerned. Whether the analogies revealed by such illustrations are indicative of some common mental habits, or whether they are part of the normal 'logic' of ornamental as well as of narrative art, is still an open question, perhaps the most challenging of all those raised by these comparisons.

a twelfth-century manuscript of the letters of St. Gregory. As for the possibilities inherent in the interlace they can be illustrated by a variety of examples from the Carolingian period onwards. The capital *B* which adorns the Second Bible of Charles the Bald (Plate VI) combines at least three different patterns of interlace. Some of the later decorated initials enable us to observe the meeting point of the interlace and the coiling spiral. While the capitals in the Albi Gradual,[1] dating from the eleventh century, merely anticipate this process of integration (Plate VII), the capital *V* from the twelfth-century Bodley manuscript of the Book of Obadiah (Plate VIII) shows the striking effects this integration could produce. Innumerable coils grow out of the main stem, so alive as to conjure up a vision of a dream-like world full of hitherto unknown living things. And even this would appear to be a relatively timid attempt beside the unbridled geometrical fancy of the Westminster Psalter (Plate IX) and of the famous Beatus initial of the Windmill Psalter (Plate X). In each of these examples the design seems to grow in complexity with every step the onlooker takes along the curves of interwoven spirals. Cohesion could hardly be carried further.[2] And yet it is not, as in classical ornament, a movement towards or away from a real or imaginary centre—since there is no centre—but towards potential infinity. The artist, like the author of a fully interlaced cyclic composition, has the entire development in mind, knows where the point of departure is for each ramification—or digression —and how to take us back, if necessary, to the line or curve we previously followed. At the same time both the artist and the cyclic romance writer see in their mind's eye endless possibilities of further growth. Hence the part assigned to unrealized movements, to themes projected into the future—or into the past. There is no limit to what a cycle might eventually receive within

[1] MS. B.N. lat. 776.
[2] The range of possible examples is wide. It includes every kind of decoration from Romanesque mural paintings to Italian wrought-iron balcony trellises. Manuscript illuminations have the advantage of enabling us to see the entire pattern at a glance on a single page. Nor is the use of the interlace in miniature painting confined to ornamental design. Plate X, illustrating a famous scene from Chrétien's *Yvain* (Yvain's encounter with Gauvain) is an example of how the same pictorial technique can be made to convey the rhythm of a single combat.

VIII. CAPITAL *V* FROM A TWELFTH-CENTURY BIBLE: first verse of the book
of Obadiah (MS. Bodl. Auct. E. inf. I, f. 281)

Photograph Bodleian Library

IX. THE BEATUS INITIAL OF THE WESTMINSTER PSALTER (late twelfth century). Brit. Mus. Royal 2 A XXII, f. 15.

its orbit, just as there is no limit to what the pictorial or sculptural ornament might absorb in its conquest of space: everything we see or read about is part of a wider canvas, of a work still unwritten, of a design still unfulfilled.

Obvious though these analogies may be, they should not be taken as evidence of a common origin, still less of an influence of one form of art upon another. The object of the comparison is simply to clarify, by mere juxtaposition, the processes at work in two parallel spheres of artistic activity. Whether or not the two phenomena can be historically related to each other is immaterial —at least for my present purpose.[1] All that really matters is to describe what there is for everyone to see. Nor is this a small undertaking. Our minds and eyes are not trained to see such things as they really are. If the Arthurian Cycle has so often been mistaken for a collection of tales haphazardly put together, it is because its mechanism is hidden behind the extraordinary complexities of the text; and if the spirals and the interlace of the decorated initials have for so long refused to yield the secret of the strictly controlled movement which they contain, it is because we have lost the art of perceiving the infinity of the great in the infinity of the small. The fascination of tracing a theme through all its phases, of waiting for its return while following other themes, of experiencing the constant sense of their simultaneous presence, depends upon our grasp of the entire structure—the most elusive that has ever been devised.

To recapture something of its rhythm we might begin by looking at a characteristic example of the interlace. One day— so the story goes in the central branch of the Cycle, the prose

---

[1] The situation is similar to that described by Jules Romains in the preface to *Les Hommes de bonne volonté* (p. xv): 'A chaque époque un des arts *autres que la littérature* se trouve particulièrement outillé pour satisfaire telle tendance dominante de la sensibilité à ce moment-là. Mais comme d'autre part, à cause de son extrême souplesse et des moyens très divers dont elle dispose, la littérature reste toujours en contact avec tous les mouvements et toutes les demandes de l'esprit; en un mot, comme elle est l'art le plus "co-extensif à l'âme humaine", il en résulte qu'elle ne laisse jamais un besoin spirituel naître ou grandir sans tâcher d'y répondre; si bien qu'à chaque époque la littérature et l'un des autres arts se rencontrent curieusement autour de préoccupations analogues, et tentent des efforts d'expression parallèles. D'où l'apparence souvent trompeuse que par cet art la littérature est influencée.'

Lancelot[1]—Arthur has a curious adventure: in a wood near Camelot he sees a wounded knight lying in a litter with two lance-heads buried in his body and a sword driven into his head. The knight begs the king to find someone who will remove the lance-heads and the sword and avenge him upon any knight who says that he loves the aggressor more than his victim. None of Arthur's knights shows any willingness to undertake such a task. At this point we are told about the arrival at Arthur's court of the Lady of the Lake with the young Lancelot who is to be dubbed knight by Arthur. Lancelot and Guinevere see each other for the first time; and as she touches his hand he trembles as if suddenly roused from sleep. After the evening service Arthur, Guinevere, and several knights go for a walk in a garden by the side of a river. Lancelot is with them, and on the way back to the palace he sees the wounded knight lying alone in a room, abandoned by all. In spite of many warnings, Lancelot, on learning the wounded knight's plight, swears to avenge him and pulls the deadly weapons from his wounds. But before he can embark upon this adventure, another adventure is announced, that of the lady of Nohant, whose castle is being besieged by the King of Northumberland. Several episodes follow, including that of the Dolorous Gard conquered by Lancelot, of Brandus des Iles whom he defeats, and of Arthur's quarrel with the King of Outre-les-Marches; at long last, after an interval which in any modern edition would occupy about a hundred pages, we are told of Lancelot's first battle on behalf of the wounded knight.[2] The theme is then abandoned again, but it keeps recurring, while in the intervals other themes rise to the surface, each broken up into comparatively short fragments, all carefully interwoven with one another, entwined, latticed, knotted, or plaited like the themes in a Romanesque ornament caught in a constant movement of endless complexity. But nothing is left to chance, and only a careless reader will find the arrangement confusing. When about eight hundred pages after the first appearance of the wounded knight and some time after the last occurrence of the theme we meet the knight again[3]

---

[1] *The Vulgate Version of Arthurian Romances*, ed. H. O. Sommer, iii. 119 ff.
[2] Ibid., pp. 174–5.   [3] Ibid. iv. 95–6.

X. THE BEATUS INITIAL OF THE WINDMILL PSALTER. MS. 102 (folio lv) of the
Pierpont Morgan Library (13th century).
By courtesy of the Pierpont Morgan Library

and discover, for the first time, that his name is Trahans le Gai, his remark: 'Je fus li chevaliers navré' is intended for those who have not forgotten any detail of the earlier episodes. The assumption is not only that the reader's memory is infallible, but that the exercise of such a memory is in itself a pleasurable pursuit which carries with it its own reward.

There are cases, however, where the reward is something more than the satisfaction of recognizing a familiar theme. The recurrence of a theme can confer fresh significance upon it, whether the theme is a statement of fact, or a description of an object, or an expression of feeling. In the course of a combat with Bors, Lancelot recognizes him by his sword:[1] it is the sword of Galehaut, which in an earlier episode—some 600 pages further back[2]—Lancelot had sent to Bors as a present. And this will be remembered again much later, in the account of Lancelot's burial at Dolorous Gard, together with the story of how Lancelot once saw there an inscription saying 'Here will lie Lancelot du Lac', and how when he heard of the death of his faithful friend Galehaut he had his body moved to Dolorous Gard, to the very place where he himself was to be buried. The symbolic ending—Lancelot's burial—at once brings home, but only to those whose memory can retain it, a whole cluster of events in their subtle succession, culminating in the tragedy of Galehaut's death. No recapitulation or reminder is needed; everything that happens remains present, firmly fixed in the mind, as if the mind's eye could absorb simultaneously all the scattered fragments of the theme, in the same way as our vision can absorb the development of motif a along the entire length of an interlaced ornament.

As an example of recurrence conveying new significance it is enough to recall the scene in which Lancelot, in the endeavour to clear Guinevere of a false accusation, has to fight single-handed three strong knights determined to destroy him.[3] In vain does

---

[1] Ibid. v. 239.　　　　　　　　　　　　　　[2] Ibid. vi. 279.

[3] Ibid. iv. 56 ff. The accusation is made by the 'false Guinevere' who says that the true Guinevere has usurped her place as the king's wife. She lures Arthur into the forest for a boar-hunt and infatuates him by her wiles. With Arthur's consent the queen is condemned to have her hair shaved off, to lose the skin of her cheeks and palms, and to be exiled for ever. Cf. E. Kennedy, 'The Two Versions of the False Guinevere Episode', in *Romania*, lxxvii. 94–104.

Arthur attempt to prevent the battle: Lancelot renounces his allegiance to Arthur and his seat at the Round Table in order to be free to prove in Arthur's court that the accusation is false: 'I release you', he says to Arthur, 'of your grace in that you made me one of your household, and from henceforth I would hold naught from you.' But as the combat is about to begin, Gawain steps forward, ties with his own hands the leather straps of Lancelot's helmet, and 'girds his sword Excalibur about Lancelot, praying him to carry it for his sake. And Lancelot said he would do so willingly'.[1] Lancelot defeats the three knights in a long and strenuous fight. He kills two of them, and before attacking the third exclaims: 'Ha, bone espee, comme il doit avoir cuer de preudhomme qui vous porte' ('Ah! great sword, he who bears you must be of noble heart').[2] Only on the queen's intercession does he spare the life of the third knight. Lancelot's victory forces Arthur to admit that the queen has been proved innocent.

The *cuer de preudhomme*, the noble heart, is Gawain's, and his gesture in giving Lancelot his own sword, Excalibur, which originally belonged to Arthur, symbolizes the depth of his affection for his friend. Once armed with *la bone espee* Lancelot knows that it will save him from defeat and the queen from dishonour. But why this gesture when Lancelot's own sword is known never to have failed him? Why should Gawain come upon the scene and say that he would 'allow no one else' to arm Lancelot?[3] The reason does not become apparent until much later, when Lancelot once more has to rescue Guinevere. In doing so he unwittingly slays the unarmed Gaheret, Gawain's brother, and Gawain's great love is turned to hate. In the ensuing struggle between the two best knights of Arthur's kingdom Excalibur appears again: it is with Excalibur that Gawain strikes Lancelot in a fierce combat in which he himself receives a fatal wound. What was once a symbol of his love for Lancelot now becomes a reminder of the

---

[1] E. Kennedy, art. cit., p. 61: 'Si li chainst messire Gauvain Escaliborc sa boine espee et li proie que pour l'amour de lui le porte. Et dist qu'il le fera moult volentiers.'

[2] Ibid., p. 64.

[3] Ibid., p. 61: 'Et si ne sueffre que nus i meist la main que seulement entr'euls deus.' Gawain may, of course, have good reasons for wanting to help Lancelot in his defence of Guinevere since he acts as her protector (cf. ibid., pp. 56, 57), but his gesture cannot be explained on these grounds alone.

broken bond between two fellow knights united by ties stronger than those of blood:

and Gawain grasped Excalibur, King Arthur's good sword, and rushed towards Lancelot and struck him with it on the head with such force that he broke his helmet.[1]

The reminder is, as always, merely implicit; but once the two events become simultaneously present in our minds, each acquires an added depth through the other and their interaction brings to the fore, as no other device could have done, the underlying tragic theme.[2]

Brevitas was in classical rhetoric one of the *virtutes narrationis*. If we are to believe what Socrates says in *Phaedrus*, the art of brevity was invented by the very founders of Greek rhetoric, Teisias and Gorgias, for purposes of judicial and political oratory, where brevity and relevance were, as indeed they still are, not only virtues, but matters of practical necessity. The story of how, through the powerful agency of Roman rhetoric, the structure of a judicial or political discourse became part of an artistic ideal has often been told, as well as the story of how, as a result, we came to believe that brevity in a work of literature was a merit and prolixity a fault; how the principle formulated by Horace in his *De Arte Poetica*—*brevis esse laboro*—came to be recognized as a universal principle of literary composition. What is not so well known is that in the medieval period the situation was very different from what it is in our own age of tame and unquestioning neo-scholasticism. Medieval treatises on the art of poetry may extol the advantages of *brevitas*, especially in narrative poetry and in the epistolary genre; but from the end of the twelfth century onwards they insist more and more on the necessity of combining *brevitas* with its converse, *dilatatio*, which is one of the forms of amplification. Curtius remarks that about the year 1200 poetic

---

[1] *La Mort le Roi Artu*, ed. Frappier, pp. 170-1.
[2] This sequence belongs to the Cycle, not to the 'short version' of the prose *Lancelot*. So far as is known (cf. E. Kennedy, art. cit., p. 104), the Cycle was an expansion of the short version, and the addition of the scene in which Gawain arms Lancelot with Excalibur was consistent with the method used throughout the Cycle.

theory offers a choice between the two procedures: an author can
draw the subject out, or he can dispatch it as briefly as possible;
and it so happens that the former method receives more attention
than the latter. The reason for this is not, as Curtius suggests,
that 'there was more to be said about *amplificatio* than about
abbreviatio',[1] but that the writers of the time, conditioned as they
were by their own literary experience, were better able than any
of their classical masters to appreciate amplification as a form of
art: not simply as a means of making the story more explicit, nor
as a concession to the reader's intellectual curiosity, but as something valuable and attractive in itself, regardless of its explanatory
function—as part of the artist's contribution to a further sophistication of the theme.

The seemingly irrational behaviour of certain Arthurian
characters is sometimes the result of this kind of elaboration.
The example that immediately comes to mind is that of Arthur's
versatile and treacherous sister, Morgan le Fay. Lucy Allen Paton
speaks of her as a character endowed with a 'wide range of capa-
cities', and Mark Twain's protagonist refers to her in equally
unequivocal terms. 'I have seen', he says, 'a good many women in
my time, but she laid them all over in variety.'

She may be [to quote Roger Sherman Loomis] Arthur's tender
nurse in the island valley of Avilion, or his treacherous foe. She may be
a virgin, or a Venus of lust. In her infinite variety she enthralled the
fancy of the Middle Ages, and has lived on to our day not only in
literature, but in folklore. As the Fata Morgana, she still evokes the
mirages of the Straits of Messina.[2]

A character whose versatility can strike with equal force three
such different observers is clearly the product of a complex
imaginative process. For Loomis, Morgan was 'manifestly a crea-
ture of tradition rather than invention'. I prefer to think that she
was both, and that in her case, as in that of many other characters

---

[1] E. R. Curtius, *Europäische Literatur und lateinisches Mittelalter* (Bern, 1948), 484:
'... begrifflicherweise widmen sie der *amplificatio* mehr Raum als der *abbreviatio*; über
jene war mehr zu sagen.'
[2] 'Morgain la fée and the Celtic goddesses', *Speculum*, vol. xx, no. 2 (Apr. 1945),
183 ff. Reprinted with some additions in *Wales and the Arthurian Legend* (Cardiff,
1956), 105–30.

of Arthurian romance, the more we can discover about the nature of the 'invention', the less likely we are to overestimate the importance of the 'tradition'.

Of particular interest is the part assigned to Morgan in the *Suite du Merlin*.[1] One day Arthur is hunting a stag in the forest of Camelot with Accalon, the lover of Morgan, and Urien, her husband.[2] The three companions see a magnificent ship gliding towards them at the river's edge, its decks hung with shining silks. They are joyfully greeted and invited to come aboard by twelve maidens who clothe them in rich attire, entertain them to a royal feast, and then take each one of them to a bedchamber. When the next day they awake they are all three in quite other places: Urien in the arms of his wife, Morgan; Arthur in a prison black as pitch; Accalon in a meadow near a spring, still wearing the robe the maidens gave him the night before. As each intrigue develops the threefold mystery becomes more and more involved. First, Accalon sees a dwarf appear in front of him in the meadow. The dwarf is carrying a sword—it happens to be Arthur's own sword—and he gives it to Accalon saying it is a gift from Morgan le Fay. When Accalon asks him to explain the meaning of it all, 'I know not,' he replies, 'save that these are the adventures of Britain, or else the enchantments of this land.'[3] And so they are; for when we next see Arthur in prison we discover that he is there because his captor needs a champion to fight for him, and Arthur agrees to take the fight upon himself in order to obtain his release and that of all the other prisoners. One of the ladies of Morgan le Fay suddenly appears at a window. She brings Arthur what he thinks is his sword; but it is only a replica: the real sword is in Accalon's hands, and it is Accalon whom Arthur has to meet in single combat the next day. He fights with all his strength, but the counterfeit weapon is soon shattered and Accalon calls upon Arthur to admit defeat. Arthur replies that he would rather die

---

[1] See above, p. 60, n. 2.
[2] *Merlin, roman en prose du XIIIᵉ siècle*, publié par Gaston Paris et Jacob Ulrich, ii. 174 ff.
[3] ' "Et comment vin ge cha? le sés tu?" "Nennil voir, che dist li nains, fors que che sont des aventures de Bretaigne ou des enchantemens de ceste terre" ' (ibid., p. 180).

than surrender; 'and he would have been killed', the author tells us, 'had it not been for the Lady of the Lake who appeared just at that moment, cast a spell upon Accalon and made the good sword drop from his hand on to the grass'.[1] Arthur seizes it, recognizes it, and tears the scabbard away from Accalon whose wounds immediately begin to bleed. For such is the magic power of the scabbard that whoever carries it can never lose a drop of blood in battle. With his last breath Morgan's unhappy lover asks Arthur to forgive his involuntary treachery: he did not know that he would be fighting his own king. Morgan's plans, however, are not so easily defeated. She tries to murder her own husband, Urien, in his sleep. Her son, Yvain, sees her approaching Urien's bed with a sword, disarms her, and threatens to kill her. As if to comfort herself for this new setback she goes to the place where Arthur is spending the night, creeps into his tent while he is asleep, and steals the magic scabbard once more from him. Arthur gives chase and Morgan, feeling her strength running out, hurls the scabbard into a lake from which it will be taken only for Gawain to wear in his fight with the sorcerer Naborn. Nothing more will be said about it at any time. Arthur will never set eyes on it again, and in the last phase of the battle of Salisbury Plain there will be no charmed weapon to prevent Mordred from wounding him to death.

Nothing quite like this series of episodes had been thought of by the authors of the 'Vulgate' Cycle. The elaborate machinations culminating in the removal of the magic scabbard from Arthur were invented by a later writer who was above all intent on producing a work that would pave the way for the main events of the *Queste del Saint Graal* and the *Mort Artu*—the two concluding branches of the Cycle. But the long succession of plots, ruses, and attempted assassinations inspired by Morgan was clearly out of all proportion to its explanatory function. Indeed, to seek its *raison d'être* in its usefulness as a preparation for the final catastrophe would be to condemn it outright. All the intrigues of Morgan

---

[1] '. . . 'il fust mors sans recouvrier, a chou qu'il se laissast anchois occhirre qu'il criast mierchi, se ne fust la damoisele dou lac, qui fu la por aidier le roi, se elle veist que Merlin n'i fust' (Paris and Ulrich (eds.), op. cit., p. 206).

outgrow—and are deliberately made to outgrow—their relevance, whether we judge their relationship to the story in dramatic or in discursive terms. How, then, are they to be justified?

So far as the story of Arthur's death is concerned, the same question may be asked with reference to some of the other seemingly superfluous additions to the original narrative. Neither Geoffrey of Monmouth[1] nor Wace[2] had tried to explain the downfall of Arthur's kingdom. To them it was a natural consequence of a military disaster—of an accident of warfare which in other circumstances could have been avoided. But as soon as the story ceased to be a chronicle and became a romance, that is to say part of the Arthurian prose cycle, it acquired a motivation of a different and characteristically complex kind.[3] The disaster was accounted for not in terms of any one major cause, but in terms of several concurrent causes. It was made clear, to begin with, that at the close of the quest for the Holy Grail divine protection had been withdrawn from Arthur and from Lancelot and that neither Arthur nor Lancelot could thenceforth save Arthurian chivalry from destruction. By classical standards this would have been an adequate explanation; but in a thirteenth-century cyclic romance there was room for more. And so the Wheel of Fortune was introduced to show that the disaster had to come in any case as a result of Arthur's rise to excessive heights of success and fame. A third line of motivation, implicit in the action and the characters, was the notion that the disaster came in the wake of divided loyalties— a theme developed in such a way as to bring out the insoluble conflict of 'two goods', one symbolized by Lancelot's allegiance to Guinevere, the other by his fidelity to Arthur and Gawain. The resulting conflict tears Arthur's kingdom apart at the moment of its gravest peril. Finally a fourth motive was added at a still later stage: Mordred, Arthur's nephew, was made the child of his incest, and Arthur's death at Mordred's hands became a retribution for his sin. It stands to reason that in order to justify this multiplication of motives and antecedents we must not think

---

[1] Ed. Edmond Faral (Paris, 1929), in *La Légende arthurienne*, iii. 274-8.
[2] Ed. Ivor Arnold (Société des Anciens Textes Français, Paris, 1940), ll. 13223-55.
[3] In *La Mort le Roi Artu*, ed. Jean Frappier (Paris, 1936), 201-26.

of them as being dramatic necessities. Not only are all of them except one redundant by the standards of classical or neo-classical dramatic composition, but their multiplicity is contrary to any recognized view of action in a novel or a play. In real life two reasons may be better than one; but if either Brutus or Othello had had more than one reason for doing what he did, the whole dramatic edifice would have collapsed like a house of cards. We are here brought face to face with a conception of artistic propriety which has little relation to any literary theory known to us. Most of us have been slow to grasp this contrast; and I confess that it was not until I came to consider the next stage in the motivation of Arthur's death—that which involves Morgan le Fay—that the nature of this process became apparent to me.

What Morgan le Fay does is to carry the process one step further, but far enough to make us realize what has been happening to the story all along. Of all Arthurian characters she is the one who conspires most consistently and most effectively against our preconceived notions of literary form. Her intrigues never spoil the story; on the contrary, they add considerably to the interest of the episodes in which they occur. But to do them justice we must recognize as legitimate one quality which they share with many other motivating themes in the Arthurian world, namely their dramatic superfluity. They are obviously even less necessary for the understanding of the tragic ending of the Arthurian epic than any one of the four themes introduced in the 'Vulgate': the Grail quest, the Wheel of Fortune, the clash of loyalties, and Arthur's incest. No less than in the case of any of these, we must think of Morgan's intrigues—if we are to understand them at all—in non-dramatic terms; preferably in pictorial terms. For what, after all, are these arabesque-like conspiracies if not an interlace practised with consummate skill? A triptych is placed before the reader at the outset: the adventure develops along three different lines until the lines begin to cross and the entire pattern converges upon the fate of the magic scabbard and that of the king himself. The resulting fabric of interwoven events is the work of a sorceress whose object is to involve us in situations of the greatest intricacy, not in order to make the final resolution of the action more acceptable, but in order to give us the kind of pleasure we experience in discovering, through patient observation, the shape of an ornament in a richly illuminated manuscript of the eleventh, twelfth, or thirteenth century.

The test of an ornament is, of course, its fitness. It must occupy a space, fulfil a purpose, be adapted to the material in which it is executed and to the process *by* which it is inserted into the general framework. Art historians tell us that while the forms of ornament are often derived from nature, repose is best secured by some remoteness from nature—some transfiguration of natural forms; for the artist's problem in ornamentation is primarily one of *design*. The same is true of the ornamental complexity of Arthurian romance. Each individual element of it may be drawn from the common stock of tradition and may even seem to conform to the pattern of ordinary human behaviour: jealousy, revenge, conflicting loyalties, human passions good or wicked, all these things may be present; but they undergo a transfiguration which for most of the late medieval writers represents the essential logic of the story: a logic of the same kind as that which brings forth the figures of animals in an inhabited scroll or the ornamental foliage growing out of the animals' heads in decorated initials, or the floral border which from the thirteenth century onwards frequently dominates the whole design of the page. These things do not have to be transparent to be enjoyed, any more than the adventures of Britain and 'the enchantments of this land'. The intricate play of shadow in the unexplored expanse of a forest of adventure is as meaningful as the light shining through the branches of 'unpathed Broceliande'. It is the magician's way of revealing this world to us—of helping us to understand how what began as an intellectual exercise, as an inquiry into the why and wherefore of seemingly indifferent events, ended as an art that

> never pales for weariness
> Of climbing heaven and gazing on the earth.

An awe-inspiring, but strangely satisfying sense of a vast design, of a continuous and constantly unfolding panorama stretching as far into the past as into the future—such are the things that hold the reader spell-bound as he progresses through these interwoven 'branches' and themes.[1] At the root of it all lies a highly developed sense of linear growth, an understanding of the great aesthetic possibilities of digression and recurrence, and the feeling of continuity and movement maintained throughout the vicissitudes of individual adventures. There is doubtless still more to it than that: the subtle balance of the two chivalries, the chivalry of the Round Table and that of the Grail; the culmination of their respective destinies in the tragic downfall of Arthur's kingdom; the unmistakable sense of the magnitude of the theme. And yet none of this could have come to life outside the setting to which it belongs. We are in an age when character has no existence outside destiny, and destiny means the convergence of simultaneously developed themes, now separated, now coming together, varied, yet synchronized, so that every movement of this carefully planned design remains charged with echoes of the past and premonitions of the future.[2]

It was this form of writing that held the whole of educated Europe spell-bound for centuries, and even when the contours became blurred the spell continued. Nothing less could have inspired the fancy of Ariosto and the dream of Don Quixote. Its eventual decline was the penalty of its very excellence. So delicate

[1] Cf. Rosemond Tuve, *Allegorical Imagery: some Medieval Books and their Posterity* (Princeton, New Jersey, Princeton University Press, 1966), 369, 370: 'As we pursue such analyses, we see that the plans of romances are not visibly dictated by that principle of subordination which governs our notions of plot, of how to outline a schema, or of how the members of a structure are articulated . . . The web is uncuttable, the delayed continuations necessary for enrichment of themes; the seeming elaborations are essential parts.' And the reason for this is that 'the unifying principle is not the *history* of a particular or an individual; the action is not a biography, a life, but an action'. Earlier on (p. 363) Rosemond Tuve makes an interesting observation which is true of some episodes, though not of all: 'Events connected by *entrelacement* are not juxtaposed; they are interlaced, and when we get back to our first character he is not where we left him as we finished his episode.' We come back 'not to precisely what we left, but to something we understand differently because of what we have seen since'.

[2] To quote again Rosemond Tuve: 'This web-structure has special possibilities of gradually discernible meaning as the woven pattern shows it *is* a pattern and *takes* shape. Hence it was a superbly invented instrument for conveying not only what we called the polyphonic nature of what is happening, but that which interested Spenser supremely, the fact that to human minds what happens "means" something, is significant' (op. cit., p. 364). The whole history of meaning and form in romance is implied in this remark.

an architecture presupposed in the reader and the writer an unusual discipline of mind and a span of attention which even in the thirteenth century could not have been the privilege of many. Already in some versions of cyclic romances dating from the second half of the century interpolations occur which are not related to what precedes or follows; and now and again some of the quests pursued by knights-errant are given up in despair. The interlace as a method and an ideal is not abandoned; it remains an inspiring model, witness the *Faerie Queene* and the revised version of Sidney's *Arcadia*, enlarged by the addition of several new stories dovetailed into the principal one.[1] Many modern critics, bred on the nineteenth-century concept of a novel, naturally prefer the cancelled *Arcadia* to the revised, forgetting that by so doing they reject a method in which generations of polished and spirited writers and readers took genuine pleasure.[2] Three hundred years after its first appearance in French cyclic romances the method not only reasserts itself, but achieves a new triumph in the work of Ariosto who describes it in apt and vivid terms:

> Di molte fila esser bisogno parme
> A condur la gran tela ch'io lavoro.[3]

Far from repudiating the medieval technique of interlace, Ariosto brings to it the resources of his rich fantasy and his consummate narrative skill; the varieties of the fabric exert upon his mind the same fascination as the varieties of tone on a musician's ear:

> Signor, far mi convien come fa il buono
> Sonator sopra il suo instrumento arguto:
> Che spesso muta corda, e varia suono,
> Ricercando ora il grave, ora l'acuto.[4]

[1] Sir Philip Sidney, *The Countess of Pembroke's Arcadia*, ed. Albert Feuillerat (Cambridge, 1922), viii.
[2] Cf. C. S. Lewis, *English Literature in the Sixteenth Century Excluding Drama* (Oxford, 1954), 332.
[3] *Orlando Furioso*, xiii. 81: 'I need many different threads to weave the wide web I labour on.' For a description of Ariosto's use of interlace see Henri Hauvette, *L'Arioste et la poésie chevaleresque à Ferrare au début du XVIᵉ siècle* (Paris, 1927), 276 ff.; Alan Gilbert's introduction to his translation of the poem (New York, 1954), xii–xxii; and Giosue Carducci, *Su Ludovico Ariosto e su Torquato Tasso* (Bologna, 1875 (?)), 295–304.
[4] Ibid. viii. 29. Hauvette (op. cit.) translates these lines as follows: [il me convient de faire] 'comme le musicien qui souvent change de corde, varie les sons, les recherche tantôt dans le registre grave et tantôt dans l'aigu.'

But while cultivating this highly sophisticated form of composition, Ariosto is equally familiar with, and equally attached to,
the less rigorous and less rational tradition which ever since the
thirteenth century had been growing out of the prose romances—
the tradition which deliberately created an impression of confusion
and emphasized the vagaries of knight-errantry, the pell-mell of
odd adventures distractedly following one another. For many
readers of the late Middle Ages and early Renaissance this kind
of disconnected 'fine-fabling' was a genuine source of delight,
and it lasted long enough to cause the tragic folly of Don Quixote,
to inspire the unpredictable flights of fancy of Boiardo's *Orlando
Innamorato*, and to create the varying moods, the music, and even
the irony of Ariosto's *Furioso*.[1] 'Romance' in the modern English
sense is a product of precisely this undisciplined trend. The term,
according to W. P. Ker, 'means almost everything—from the two
horsemen riding together at the beginning of the historical
novel, or from the pasteboard Moors of the puppet-show to
the spell of the enchanted ground, the music of dreams and
shadows'.[2] As a narrative form, Romance affords the story-teller
an opportunity to achieve suspense in the midst of complex
situations, and it is in order to safeguard this opportunity that
in eighteenth-century England writers like Hurd attempted a
justification of things which were popularly condemned as
Gothic and fanciful. Fairy-tales in Tasso's work were, Hurd
thought, greater than the 'classical parts': 'We make a shift to
run over the passages he has copied from Virgil. We are all on

[1] The problem of the structure of *Orlando* is more complex than it might appear
from these brief remarks. Carducci (op. cit.) speaks of Ariosto's *potenza d'ordinamento*
and quotes in support Panizzi's analysis of the poem; and Panizzi in his turn quotes
Charles Fox who, he tells us, 'was wont to say that the *Orlando Furioso* was the most
regular and connected of all the poems he knew'. 'It is easy', he remarks, 'to laugh
at the words *unity of action*, but the fact is that without a thread with which to trace
his way through the story, without some person in view with which [sic] all the
events are more or less connected, it is impossible even for the reader to enjoy the
perusal of the poem.' He finds this kind of unity not only in the *Furioso*, but in Pulci's
Morgante: the flights of fancy are, he thinks, controlled in both works by a skilful
grouping of characters around the protagonist and of the various 'threads' which
all culminate in a single denouement. Cf. his *Life of Ariosto*, in vol. i of his ed.
of the *Furioso* (pp. xiv ff.), and his essay on Boiardo and Ariosto (London, 1830),
233.
[2] W. P. Ker, *Romance* (English Association, Pamphlet no. 19, Mar. 1909), 12.

fire amidst the magical feats of Ismen, and the enchantments of Armida.'[1]

At the other end of the scale there was then, as there had been since the last centuries of the Middle Ages, a strong resistance to 'fine-fabling' of either kind—controlled or uncontrolled. The strictures of Don Quixote's friend, the canon of Toledo, and his violent reaction to what he thought were the absurdities and incoherences of the romances of chivalry, stem from an instinctive knowledge of the deeper tendencies of his own age. He thought the romances were composed 'in such a way that one could never find one's way about them': in some cases this was true; but whether the incoherences were real or merely apparent was immaterial to a reader as unwilling as he was to be involved in structural complexities. The ideal form of narrative for such a reader was the *novella*—a short tale with a single theme, capable of crystallizing a particular situation around a few summarily drawn characters.[2] Recent studies have shown that what gave the genre its original impetus in France was not simply the influence of Boccaccio's *Decameron*, but a spontaneous reaction against 'interlaced' composition.[3] Long before the French *nouvelle* reached the status which it was to enjoy in the fifteenth century, self-contained stories began to occur within the framework of certain cycles.[4] And even though these stories often remained embedded in voluminous cyclic manuscripts,[5] they were to all intents and purposes the natural prototypes of the *nouvelle*, characterized by the singleness of the theme and the simplicity of the narrative design. It was a process of segmentation—destructive and creative at the same time—changing a well-established form into its very opposite: the longest conceivable type of story into the shortest, and the most complex into the

[1] Quoted by W. P. Ker, ibid., p. 2.
[2] So defined by Janet M. Ferrier in her *Forerunners of the French Novel* (Manchester, 1934, p. 31), the most significant recent study of the problem.
[3] Cf. ibid. in ch. i, the structural analysis of the *nouvelle* and its antecedents.
[4] Cf. ibid., pp. 20-1: 'Types of emphasis familiar to the readers of *Cent Nouvelles Nouvelles* are traceable to certain detachable fragments of these romances.'
[5] An interesting example of this process is MS. B.N. fr. 112 produced by the famous fifteenth-century scribe Michel Gonnot. On its importance for the history of medieval narrative technique see C. E. Pickford, *L'Évolution du roman arthurien vers la fin du moyen âge d'après le ms. 112 du fonds français de la Bibliothèque Nationale* (Paris, 1960).

simplest. Once enlivened by such writers as Marguerite de Navarre and Thomas Nash, who grafted upon it their own methods of characterization, the new form became in all essentials that of the modern novel. The subsequent expansion of the scale left it virtually intact.

One of our most misleading modern assumptions is that intellectual and spiritual values move about on their own in a kind of disorganized space, occasionally choosing for themselves a particular form of artistic expression. When we think of 'characterization' in a work of narrative we usually imagine that it comes to the artist as a result of some process prior to, or even unconnected with, the work in hand, stimulated by experience or speculation. Whatever the value of this theory as an interpretation of certain varieties of modern fiction, it applies neither to medieval narrative nor, if we are to believe the more recent art historians, to medieval visual arts. In both these fields delineation of character, if it exists at all, is determined, as it were, *from within*, by fundamental changes of *form*. In Romanesque sculpture the figures are usually so placed as to feel, or appear to feel, the full pressure of a vast architectural ensemble: they seem to pull against their frame as if they wished to loosen its hold upon them. In reality, they attempt nothing of the kind: they adapt themselves with admirable precision to the contours and the scale of the building;[1] they live and have their being within the space created for them by the artist.[2] And so it is with a cyclic romance, each element of which,

[1] Cf. Henri Focillon, *L'Art des sculpteurs romans: recherches sur l'histoire des formes* (Paris, 1931), 274: 'L'art roman est une série d'expériences sur la mobilité. Par leurs saillants les figures s'appuient contre leurs cadres et, soumises à l'architecture, elles s'arc-boutent comme si elles tentaient vraiment de s'en affranchir. Mais elles s'y plient avec exactitude, elles en épousent le dessin et les proportions. Elles jonglent, elles dansent, elles nagent dans un univers qu'elles n'excèdent jamais.'

[2] Cf. Jurgis Baltrušaitis, *La Stylistique ornementale dans la sculpture romane* (Paris, 1931), 275: 'L'artiste roman crée des corps nouveaux en changeant les proportions et souvent l'aspect même de leurs membres. C'est en visant l'exactitude du schéma et non pas la ressemblance avec la nature qu'il compose le relief de ces bêtes . . . Ce sont des animaux fantastiques, toute une faune inédite, qui habitent désormais les forêts et les labyrinthes du décor architectural. Ainsi la déformation ornementale crée des monstres. Quand son activité s'accroît, quand elle maîtrise complètement son sujet, quand elle décompose radicalement un corps, cette déformation est formation. C'est la création immédiate de la matière figurée. L'image émane en quelque sorte de la structure ornementale.'

XI. CHARTRES CATHEDRAL. FIGURES FROM THE CENTRAL PORCH OF THE
WEST FRONT, *ca.* 1150 (three kings and a queen of Judah)
Photograph James Austin

XII. CHARTRES CATHEDRAL. FIGURES FROM THE CENTRAL PORCH OF THE
SOUTH FRONT, *ca.* 1260 (Saint Martin, Saint Jerome, and Saint Gregory)

Photograph James Austin

with all its ramifications, is fashioned and controlled by the pattern of the cycle as a whole. The determining factor in both cases is the *setting*: the ornamental context of the building in one case and the narrative context of a romance of chivalry in the other. And just as the transition from Romanesque to Gothic sculpture is essentially a process of liberation from architectural space,[1] so in the rebuilding of cyclic romances the decisive moment is the feeling that a story can live its own life, unrestrained by the structural dialectic which gave it its original form, and free to seek motivation in its own substance, to discover its own centre of gravity and its own frame of reference. In the Royal Portal at Chartres (1145–50) the statues are still an integral part of the structure:[2] their whole being is determined by the architectural design and the setting in which they are placed. But the sculpture of the next century in the same cathedral[2] shows the human figure regaining its autonomy. The same development can be observed in the north and south transepts of Westminster Abbey.[4] The figures of the angels symbolically enclosed in ornamental patterns, their wings at first barely showing, witness the awakening of a new concept of sculptural decoration. The prevailing impression may still be that of the original block of stone out of which heads, arms, and folds have been carved. Yet some of the figures mark a decisive step in the direction of total emancipation. Although the angels lean upon the arch, they no longer seem to be part of it: some of them barely touch the arch with one knee, as if they had inadvertently brushed the surface of it as they flew in from outer space. The process will be completed when the human figures that once served as pillars or ornamental devices arrange themselves in groups possessing each its own visible centre and its own *raison d'être*.[5] This gradual and remarkably

---

[1] Of the sculptures at Saint-Denis Focillon says: 'Ils quittent l'espace de l'architecture pour venir à nous, dans l'espace vrai, où ils pénètrent de face et non de biais' (op. cit., p. 270). Cf. also his description in the same chapter of the Nativity group in the church of La Charité-sur-Loire.

[2] See Pl. XI.   [3] See Pl. XII.   [4] See Pls. XIII and XIV.

[5] Henri Focillon, op. cit., pp. 220–1: 'Les statues-colonnes cessent d'évoquer une fonction portante, se détachent du mur ou du piédroit [. . .] Le mouvement de nouveau les parcourt et les anime, mais ce sont les flexions de la vie et non plus les flexions d'ornement.'

consistent change is a clear prefiguration of the interplay of plot and character within the well-defined limits of a work of fiction as conceived by late medieval writers. Art, modelling itself on nature, discovers at each stage of its evolution new sources of creative energy.[1] Yet it is different from nature in that potentially it still is whatever it has been. The 'twisted eglantine' never vanishes; receding into the background as if its spells were only broken for a time, it remains ready to return and twist with renewed vigour

> the chains that tie
> The hidden soul of harmony.

And when, in a thrust against the functional, the rational, and the straightforward, poetic form in our modern age proclaims its own autonomous value,[2] when it discards those other, much heavier, chains known as simplicity, brevity, and singleness, who can say that the discoveries of the past have been lost, or that the meeting-point between the Middle Ages and ourselves has not at long last been reached?

---

[1] As long ago as 1596 Gioseppe Malatesta suggested a more compact way of describing this same phenomenon: '. . . Il presumersi dell' arti fermezza alcuna, non che perpetuità di stato, è un presumersi constante l'inconstanza medesima' (quoted by Bernard Weinberg, op. cit., p. 1062).

[2] In his epoch-making work entitled *Le Temps de la Contemplation* (Paris, 1969), Professor Jean Gaudon has shown that in French poetry this insurrection can be traced at least as far back as Victor Hugo. He writes: 'A partir d'un certain point d'exaltation lyrique, la décoration devenue sa propre raison d'être . . . impose à l'œuvre un nouveau mode de structuration. Elle se fait agression contre ce qu'elle avait charge d'embellir, agression furieuse contre le fonctionnel, le rationnel, le rectiligne. Elle est prolifération inutile, mouvement passionnel, fourmillement. Elle est ce gigantesque paradoxe: un artifice qui introduisit dans l'art le seul naturalisme véritable' (p. 101).

XIII. FIGURE OF AN ANGEL in the north transept of Westminster Abbey

XIV. FIGURE OF AN ANGEL in the south transept of Westminster Abbey

VI

ANALOGY AS THE DOMINANT FORM

LIKE the spirals adorning a painted initial the lines of inquiry we have so far been pursuing now divide themselves, giving rise to two distinct types of convolution. One of them follows chronologically the sequence of the changing forms of fiction, the other embraces literary events similar in character but sometimes widely separated in time and space. Whichever of these approaches we adopt now, we shall eventually have to return to our point of departure. The 'atemporal' approach—the more adventurous of the two—ought perhaps to be tried first.

From the intrusion of meaning upon matter down to the elaboration of narrative sequences in cyclic romances, what we have observed is a series of attempts to establish a causal order within the narrative. As E. M. Forster has it, the author in such cases is 'poised above' the story, 'throwing a beam of light here, popping a cap of invisibility there'.[1] For the early examples of medieval narrative the 'beam of light' would be a more appropriate image than the cap of invisibility. Romance writers like Chrétien de Troyes do nothing to conceal their intentions or to deny the superiority of their narrative technique over the crude habits of those ignorant story-tellers who go about reciting tales *devant rois et devant comtes* in a disjointed and, as Chrétien would say, 'corrupt' fashion. Chrétien had good reason to be proud of his skill as a rhetorician; his method of work is still considered valid; poets and prose writers are still expected, whenever they try to put the action of a novel or a play into reasonable shape, to build it upon the notion of a sequence in which the events of the story become intelligible in terms of whatever may have caused them to occur. But just as in thirteenth-century theology each *summa* supplied a variety of ways in which divine truth could be

[1] *Aspects of the Novel*, p. 92.

apprehended, so in the art of literary composition different approaches to the understanding of any given subject were allowed and sometimes even required. The idea that to multiply the foundations of faith is to strengthen it is obviously not a universal one; but it was widely accepted both by medieval theologians and by twelfth- and thirteenth-century writers of fiction who firmly believed that they could make the events they described appear more credible and more significant if they could lead up to them in a variety of ways.

We are only now beginning to realize the extent and the nature of the various procedures they employed—the direction of the mysterious 'lines of force' operating in the field of medieval fiction; but we have already noticed that certain events become intelligible to us regardless of what may or may not have *caused* them to occur. Balin does not cause the advent of Galahad: he simply confers a deeper significance upon it by acting as the embodiment of the dark forces which Galahad is to dispel. This is one of the clearest cases of analogy supplying all the necessary preparation.[1] We know how widespread at that time was the use made by theologians of arguments from analogy—arguments based on the belief that the universe formed an ordered structure of such a kind that the pattern of the whole was reproduced in the pattern of the parts, and that inferences from one category of phenomena to the other were therefore valid methods of approach for the understanding of either. In a famous passage of his *Summa contra Gentiles* Thomas Aquinas explains that since we cannot, in speaking of God and the creatures, use the same terms either in an identical or in a totally different sense, we must use them analogically. He was well aware that the *feeling* for the analogical approach transcended any particular school of thought and was shared by most medieval thinkers from St. Augustine onwards. Christ, according to St. Augustine, is called Divine Light properly, not figuratively—not in terms of a distinction between physical and transcendental light, but because of the analogy of the two lights.

---

[1] It is an almost universal belief in primitive society that to imitate an event is to bring it to pass (cf. John Murphy, *Lamps of Anthropology* (Manchester, 1943), 73). The device of analogy in art has the same psychological foundation.

Such an analogy is neither a mere poetical play nor an allegorical illustration, but a means of apprehending the Divine Presence, a valid approach to knowledge and understanding.[1] Just as in the light of day that filters through the rose window of a cathedral and illumines the sanctuary, mystical reality becomes palpable to the senses,[2] so in a composition which, for lack of a better term, we describe as developing on two or more 'levels', the need for ultimate conviction is fulfilled, the enriched concord achieved, and with it a total form—the form that has endless possibilities of foreshadowings and prefigurations and grows in significance each time it brings an echo of a half-remembered, yet living past:

> . . . un écho redit par mille labyrinthes,
> Un ordre renvoyé par mille porte-voix.

Balin is fated not only to lay waste two kingdoms by his Dolorous Blow, but to die in a fratricidal combat after having inflicted mortal wounds upon his own brother Balan whom he will fail to recognize. Throughout the story a strange sense of foreboding is borne in upon us, not through a consistently developed plot, but by means of successive prefigurations of the theme of fratricide. When a knight entrusted to Balin's care is killed by an invisible hand Balin exclaims: 'Shame upon me in whose care this knight has been struck dead.' When he rides with another knight they enter a graveyard and the knight suddenly cries out: 'Ah, my friend, I am dead, for I have stayed too long in your company.' He too has been murdered by an invisible hand, and as Balin looks at him lying dead he says to himself that he is the unhappiest man that ever wore armour, for 'Fortune is more hostile to him than to any living man.' And so until the end of the Balin story, as mischance pursues him and dogs his steps, the final catastrophe is brought more and more within our field of vision like a shadow that grows with each step we take. In James Joyce's *Portrait of the Artist* Stephen Dedalus says that terror in tragedy 'is the feeling

---

[1] Cf. *De Genesi ad literam*, iv. 28. Figurative references to divinity form, according to St. Augustine, a separate class. To call Christ 'the Keystone' is to describe Him symbolically, not analogically. Cf. Étienne Gilson, *The Spirit of Medieval Philosophy*, p. 100.

[2] Cf. Otto von Simson, *The Gothic Cathedral* (New York, 1962), *passim*.

which arrests the mind in the presence of whatsoever is grave and constant in human sufferings and *unites it with the secret cause*'. Tragedy for him demands the awareness of this unfathomable order of things, of what Aristotle called the 'appearance of design'. What Stephen Dedalus does not say is that this sense of the 'secret cause', of the hidden relationship of things, can only be conveyed to us by means which defy analysis, at a moment when the visible and the rational are powerless to provide the illumination we are seeking. The apprehension of a crushing blow of fate cannot be achieved by a consistently motivated series of events; it calls for antecedents of a different order, for reasons similar to those which enable man to ascend from the world of shadows and images to the contemplation of spiritual things—reasons unknown to any form of discursive reasoning. This is how Balin's own tragic end is brought about. And if we now look at Balin's passage across Arthur's kingdom in the wider perspective of the entire Cycle, we shall find that it bears a close analogical relationship to the two most significant events of the vast epic of the Round Table. As a necessary counterpart to Galahad, Balin heralds his coming; and at the same time his own tragedy of fratricide sets the scene for the destruction of Arthur's kingdom—for the struggle between Gawain and Lancelot, the two noblest knights who between them symbolize the greatness and the glory of the entire Arthurian fellowship. Their feud is the outcome of tensions inherent in the acceptance of the most exalted mode of feeling and living ever devised; and it is only through a carefully built-up series of warnings, premonitions, and symbolically similar manifestations of human destiny that we can accede to the comprehension of a catastrophe which springs from the very source of all human greatness.

In Geoffrey of Monmouth's *Historia Regum Britanniae* and in its French adaptation by Wace, Arthur has a sword called *Caliburnus* which on many occasions stands him in good stead.[1] And yet

---

[1] Identified by Heinrich Zimmer with the Irish Caladbolg. But while Caladbolg could on occasion become the size of a rainbow and cut off the top of a hill, no such virtues are ascribed to Caliburnus, and the fact that, as Zimmer points out, both swords are used in battle 'in decisive moments' is clearly of no significance. A much

the very first time this sword appears in romance it is Arthur's
no more.[1] In Chrétien's *Conte del Graal* it belongs to Arthur's
nephew Gawain,[2] and Chrétien does not even say how Gawain
came to be its possessor. The real reason for the change is, of
course, the eclipse of Arthur in the French courtly romances of the
twelfth century. In these romances the chronicle of Arthur's
campaigns and battles was replaced by stories of the adventures
of his knights, and there was little left for him to do save to preside
over his court when adventures were begun or concluded. 'The
best sword that ever was'—now called Excalibur—naturally had
to be taken away from the benevolent but idle king and placed
in more active hands. But when in the thirteenth century the
chronicle material came to be revived and a whole new branch
dealing with the early history of Arthur's kingdom—the *Estoire
de Merlin*—was added to the cycle of romances, the question
arose as to how the two traditions could be reconciled: how the
sword could be restored to Arthur and yet remain Gawain's.

The answer was found in a device meaningless by traditional
modern standards of cogency, but entirely adequate from the
thirteenth-century point of view. Halfway through the *Estoire de
Merlin* a new incident was introduced: Gawain's investiture by
Arthur. Arthur makes Gawain constable of the kingdom and the
next day, in the palace of Logres, knights him with his good sword
Excalibur. 'So King Arthur took the sword which by Merlin's
design he had drawn from the stone, and he girt it about Gawain,
his nephew. And then he attached the right spur and King Ban
the left.'[3] The sword with which a feudal lord arms his vassal is

more likely model is the Latin word *chalybs*, the poetical term for steel or sword used
by Virgil in a passage which was well known to Geoffrey (*Aeneid*, viii. 446). Cf.
Edmond Faral, *La Légende arthurienne*, ii. 226, and my article on 'King Arthur's Sword'
in the *Bulletin of the John Rylands Library*, vol. xl, no. 2, p. 516.

[1] In Wace's *Brut* Arthur's sword is mentioned five times (ll. 9279, 10083, 11547,
12910, 12926), but only once without Geoffrey's support, and always in the same
terms as in Geoffrey.

[2] Ed. W. Roach, ll. 5903–4:

La meillor espee qui fust,
Qu'elle trenche fer come fust.

[3] *The Vulgate Version of the Arthurian Romances*, ed. H. O. Sommer, ii. 253: 'Si prinst
li rois Artus sa boine espee qu'il osta del perron par le conseil Merlin, si la pent a
Gavaine son neveu al costé, et puis li caucha l'esperon destre et li rois Bans le senestre.'

both a token of the vassal's obligations and the means by which these obligations are to be discharged. Hence, even though Arthur 'gives' Excalibur to Gawain, Excalibur remains the emblem and the instrument of Arthur's power. The apparent ambiguity of the theme is mitigated by the familiar ambivalence of the feudal bond. And in order to dispose of the ambiguity altogether and secure Arthur's claim to the sword, the author places the scene of Gawain's investiture in such a way as to divide the *Estoire de Merlin* into two equal halves,[1] each inaugurated, as it were, by Excalibur. The second half begins with Gawain becoming a knight through Excalibur; the first, with Arthur becoming a king through Excalibur when he draws it from the stone.[2] The two scenes are symmetrical in position and parallel in content. In a thirteenth-century cyclic romance such an arrangement inevitably created the impression that whatever happened on the first occasion was somehow re-enacted on the second: everything remained present throughout the story, and a brief reference, sometimes a single phrase or a seemingly casual allusion, sufficed to bring back what was said in a parallel passage, however remote. Gawain's investiture recalls all that occurred at the time of Arthur's coronation—how Arthur received his crown from the archbishop, how he swore to protect the Church and to govern the kingdom justly and loyally, and how in token of this he once more took the sword out of the stone and placed it upon the altar.[3] And even as we watch Gawain receive Excalibur from Arthur, the vision of this earlier and greater scene is drawn into the foreground, making the link between Arthur and his sword into a sacred bond which no human agency can break.

[1] In Sommer's edition (op. cit.) this occurs exactly 166 pages after the end of Robert de Borron's *Merlin* and 166 pages before the death of King Rions, which concludes the *Estoire de Merlin* proper. The two halves of the *Estoire* run respectively from p. 88 to p. 253 and from p. 254 to p. 419.

[2] This famous incident is part of the prose version of Robert de Borron's *Merlin* incorporated in the *Merlin* branch of the 'Vulgate' Cycle. In Geoffrey's *Historia* there is no need for any such miracle because Arthur is considered the legitimate son of Uther Pendragon: only Merlin and Uther know that he was conceived a few hours before Uther married Igerna. In Robert de Borron the marriage takes place two months later, with the result that when Arthur is born he has to be taken away from the palace and entrusted to the care of Antor (Auctor) and his wife who bring him up as their own child. The miracle of the sword thus becomes the only effective means of establishing Arthur's claim to the throne.   [3] *The Vulgate Version*, ii. 85.

As we follow the elaboration of Arthurian romance in the thirteenth century, more examples of this kind come to our notice: examples of how the juxtaposition of analogous incidents can be used as a means of bringing to light something which would otherwise have remained unknown or unexplained. The result is a widening of the forms of 'understanding', paralleled in the history of contemporary religious thought, and more especially in the use of the symbolic method of persuasion which was held to be as effective as the most rigorous logical demonstration. In the words of M.-D. Chenu,[1] 'in the second half of the twelfth century, the growing diffusion of the great work of pseudo-Dionysius, as transmitted by John the Scot, provided a theory and practice of the symbol of a wholly different character from those of the Latin tradition [. . .] Connatural with matter, a man's intelligence had to work through matter to attain a grasp of transcendent realities, unknowable in themselves'. The symbol was the means by which these realities could be approached; being homogeneous with them, it supplied a meaningful analogy. Secular prose and poetry followed the same pattern of elucidation, except that for the theological *anagoge*, or the upward reference to things, it substituted a horizontal reference from one theme to another.

At the close of the battle of Salisbury Plain, when Arthur suffers his first and last defeat, he orders his sword to be cast into a near-by lake. A hand rises above the water to receive it. In Malory's words,

there came an arm and a hand above the water, and took it and cleyght[2] it, and shook it thrice and brandished it, and then vanished with the sword into the water.

There is a sense of wonder about this ending, which the Arthurian Prose Cycle itself—the so-called Vulgate—does not even attempt to explain. That Arthur should have wished his sword to vanish from sight before he died was as understandable as Roland's desire to break his sword Durendal lest it should fall into a Saracen's hands. But was it not enough to let Excalibur sink to the bottom of the lake and remain there for ever? Why should a mysterious

[1] M.-D. Chenu, *Nature, Man and Society in the Twelfth Century* (Chicago and London, 1957), 123.
[2] = seized.

arm come out of the water and remove Arthur's sword beyond the boundaries of any human kingdom?

Some such question must have occurred to the prose writer who composed the most remarkable of all the continuations of the 'Vulgate' Cycle, the *Suite du Merlin*, which, as we now know, was originally conceived not simply as a factual addition to the Cycle, but as an elucidation of some of its themes; and one of the themes it attempted to elucidate was precisely that of Arthur's sword. With this in mind the author added a series of incidents supposed to have taken place soon after Arthur's coronation. The newly crowned king, armed with the sword which he has drawn from the stone, challenges an unknown knight who dwells in a forest. In a long and fierce combat Arthur is unhorsed and his sword splintered to pieces against that of his opponent. He is saved by the timely arrival of Merlin. Another sword must now be found for him, and it must be strong enough to last him all his life. Merlin leads Arthur to the edge of a lake; from the depths of the water rises an arm in a sleeve of rich silk holding a sword in its hand. A mysterious lady appears coming from the sea shore. She crosses an invisible bridge to reach the centre of the lake, takes the sword, and gives it to Arthur. It is this sword which will henceforth bear the name of Excalibur.[2] And when the king's last hour comes, the hand that held the sword above the water will receive it from him, and restore it to the enchanted place it came from: the epic of Excalibur will have come full circle.

To find out how this story came to be composed we need look no further than the author's desire to make the episode of the sword not only *understandable*, but *inevitable*, to establish between the first appearance of the sword and its return to its mysterious bearer a continuity which would make the supernatural a necessary part of all that happens to Arthur's kingdom from the day of its foundation.[3] As August-Wilhelm Schlegel says in another connec-

---

[1] See Fanni Bogdanow, *The Romance of the Grail, passim.*

[2] In a passage reproduced from the *Estoire de Merlin* in the Cambridge MS. of the *Suite*, which probably represents an earlier version of the work than does the Huth MS., the sword drawn from the anvil is also called Escalibor (fol. 206 recto, col. 1). The inconsistency reappears in Malory's *Tale of King Arthur.*

[3] Something of the original continuity is sacrificed in the process, for the sword which vanishes is no longer the one which Arthur drew from the anvil and which

tion, 'an isolated miracle astonishes, but does not move; it is when the miracle becomes *part of the order of things* that it acquires its power to move'.[1] In the continuation of the 'Vulgate' Cycle the appearance of the hand which receives the sword is not an incidental intrusion of magic upon Arthur's world. The skilful repetition in reverse accompanied by a darkening of the tone gives shape and movement to the entire sequence: the two phases of Arthur's destiny, by their contrast of light and shade, amplify and enrich each other like contrasting voices in a choral fugue.

It is instructive to watch the growth of this kind of coherence from one work to another.[2] In the so-called 'First Continuation' of Chrétien's *Perceval* the same writer found a curious adventure. Queen Guinevere sends Gawain to fetch an unknown knight whom Kay has failed to bring to court. While the knight is riding in Gawain's *conduit* he dies, exclaiming, 'I have been killed in your charge!' The murderer is never found, and suspicion naturally falls on Kay.[3] Another continuator of the *Conte del Graal* elaborates the story further. The dead knight's sister urges Gawain to avenge his death. Gawain then rides to Carduel where he finds Kay serving at the king's table, and defeats him in single combat.[4]

It was from this material that the author of the *Suite du Merlin*, or, as it may now be called, the *Roman du Graal*, extracted the two examples of *mescheance* that I have already mentioned in passing. First, a knight riding with Balin is killed by an invisible hand holding a lance. 'In an evil hour', he exclaims, 'did I trust you to protect me'. Balin looks back and sees him lying on the ground:

secured his accession to the throne. In the *Coming of Arthur* Tennyson ingeniously reconciles the two traditions:

> I beheld Excalibur
> Before him at his crowning borne, the sword
> That rose from out the bosom of the lake.

[1] 'Un miracle isolé se concilie plus difficilement l'imagination que tout un ordre de choses où les miracles sont habituels' (*Comparaison de la Phèdre de Racine et celle d'Euripide* (Paris, 1807), 95).

[2] I reproduce here the substance of part of my introduction to *Le Roman de Balain* (ed. M. D. Legge (Manchester, 1942)).

[3] Cf. *The Continuations of the Old French* Perceval *of Chrétien de Troyes*, ed. William Roach and Robert H. Ivy, ii (Philadelphia, 1950), ll. 16818–17043.

[4] Cf. *Perceval le Gallois ou le Conte du Graal*, ed. Ch. Potvin (Paris, 1865–6), ll. 37431 ff.

et quant il est venus a lui, il trueve qu'il est ferus par mi le cors d'une glaive si durement que li fiers li passe tout outre par mi le cors. Lors est tant dolans que nus plus, si dist: 'Ha! Dieus, honnis sui quant chis est ensi mors en men conduit!'[1]

When another knight riding in Balin's company is struck by the same invisible hand, and Balin sees him lying dead, the description of his grief is made more poignant still by the use of repetition with variation:

Et lors recommence son duel aussi grant comme a l'autre fie. Et dist qu'il est li plus chetis et li plus mescheans chevaliers de tous cheus qui onques portaissent armes; car ore voit il apertement que fortune li est plus contraire et plus anemie que a nul autre houme.'[2]

At length he finds the murderer, Garlan, whose part in the story is similar to that of Kay in the 'Continuation'; like Kay, he is found in a royal castle serving at table. But although (unlike Kay) he is the real murderer, his death does not bring the story to a happy conclusion: it leads to yet another and still greater calamity, for Garlan's brother, Pelleham, challenges Balin, and Balin strikes him with a sacred weapon. The bright and smiling landscape of Arthur's realm, as Chrétien saw it, vanishes; and in its place we find the sorrowful land, *la terre gastee*, blighted by Balin's Dolorous Stroke.

Until the end of the Balin story his *mescheance* pursues its relentless course, aided at each stage by the author's skill in adapting his borrowings to his design. An episode already summarized in Chapter IV above forms an integral part of this sequence. Balin meets a knight who is anxiously awaiting his beloved; they set out together to look for her and find her in the arms of another man. The knight draws his sword and in a fit of rage kills the two lovers. But when he realizes what he has done he stabs himself to death and cries out with his last breath:

Ha! las, que ai jou fait qui ai mon cuer et ma dame mis a mort, cele par cui je vivoie et dont totes mes joies venoient?

The episode is reminiscent of an adventure involving Gawain and a 'sorrowful knight' in the 'First Continuation' of *Perceval*,

---

[1] *Le Roman de Balain*, ed. M. D. Legge, Manchester 1942, p. 45.
[2] Ibid., p. 57.

except that in that poem Gawain, who plays a part similar to Balin's, forces the lady's lover to surrender her to the *pensis chevaliers*, and all ends well. How little Balin resembles his more famous prototype can be seen from his poignant lament over his *male mescheance*:

'Ceste male aventure est plus avenue par male meskeanche que par autre chose; car sans faille je sui li plus mescheans chevaliers qui soit, si est bien esprouvé et chi et aillours.'

The denouement of Balin's adventures is a conflation of the motif of fratricide with an episode borrowed from *Méraugis de Portlesguez*. Méraugis comes to a castle and hears the blowing of horns. He wonders what this means, for in his own country the horns were only blown before the kill.[1] Similarly, when Balin comes within three bowshots of the castle he hears the sound of horns and asks himself what it is. 'If they blow the horns for the kill, am I the prey?' There is a melancholy foreboding in these words. Balin almost expects the fate that awaits him, a nuance totally unknown to *Méraugis*. The subsequent episodes are equally characteristic: like Balin, Méraugis discovers that the custom of the castle obliges him to challenge a knight who lives on a near-by island. The knight turns out to be his dearest friend, Gawain, and the combat comes to an abrupt end as soon as the two friends have recognized each other. Not so with the ill-fated Balin. Before the battle he changes his shield and so seals his doom, for only by his shield could he have been recognized. His opponent turns out to be more than a friend: it is his brother Balan, and so strong is the tie of blood between them that when Balin sees him preparing for battle he cannot help being half aware of the truth: *Ensi li dist ses cuers vraies nouvelles de son frere*. In *Méraugis* recognition puts an end to the battle; in *Balain* the discovery comes too late. The two brothers, mortally wounded, can only comfort themselves with the thought that they will be united in death as they were in life and that their deaths will be a worthy object of pity:

li preudomme et li boin chevalier plaindront nos mesqueanches pour la boine chevalerie et pour les biaus fais qu'il orront conter de nous.

[1] Raoul de Houdenc, *Méraugis de Portlesguez*, ed. Friedwagner (Halle, 1897), ll. 2859–73.

The catastrophe is brought about in no rational manner, by means of significant parallels. For tragedy does not exist where a sinner is punished according to his deserts or an offence duly expiated. 'Such a story', to quote again an Aristotelian formula, 'would move us to neither pity nor fear: pity is occasioned by undeserved misfortune, and fear by that of one like ourselves.' Neither is aroused by an equitable adjustment of the hero's fate to his deed. These emotions find their way to works of narrative through a sense of the futility of the noblest endeavour in face of the uncontrollable forces which govern man's destiny; they are brought home when the tragic doom is deepened by the shadows which destiny casts upon the whole range of human life. No rational explanation relieves the gloom of Balin's fate, no comfort exists for his *mescheance*, and no reason for his death, beyond the remarkable recurrence of the tragic pattern. When Balin learns that his opponent is his beloved brother he cannot speak, and falls as though he were dead. And when his brother unlaces Balin's helm to look at his mortal wounds he can hardly recognize him:

car il avoit le viaire taint de sanc et de suour, et les ieus clos et enflés, et la bouce plainne de limon et d'escume toute ensanglentee . . . 'Ha! biau frere, quele mesaventure chi a! . . . Onques si grant mesqueanche n'avint a deus freres coume il nous est avenue!'

In this final scene all the earlier events acquire an added meaning, as if several faint visions superimposed one upon another served to illumine the last and greatest of them.

An example drawn from medieval hagiography will show how closely even the least sophisticated forms of thirteenth-century narrative follow this pattern of structure. Many brief accounts of saints' lives must have been in circulation before they were incorporated in such collections as Vincent de Beauvais' *Speculum historiale*[1] and Jacobus a Voragine's *Legenda Aurea*.[2] It is customary

---

[1] The last section of a vast encyclopedia of universal knowledge entitled *Speculum maius*. Part of it was edited by O. Holder-Egger in *Monumenta Germaniae Historica*, vol. xxiv (1879).

[2] Composed between 1255 and 1266. It received its title at a later date as a compliment to its standard character. The last complete edition is still that published by Graesse in 1850.

to describe the Latin *vitae* contained in these collections as 'epitomes', but the term is misleading. In a number of cases these short *vitae* precede the longer and more elaborate retellings of the same legends:[1] the narrative tends to grow rather than diminish in size; the content is expanded, sequences of incidents are lengthened, and certain historical and geographical details added so as to give the story the appearance of a genuine chronicle. Most saints' lives seem to have developed along the same lines as the romances, but perhaps the most complete parallel to the processes outlined in the preceding pages is found in the story of St. Julian, the patron saint of travellers, known as St. Julian the Hospitaller. In the earliest version only the barest account is given of how Julian killed his parents and did penance for his crime: *predixit ei quidam quod parentes esset occissurus.*[2] The emphasis is on the punishment meted out to the sinner and on the sinner's rise to sainthood, in other words on the *consequences* of the central event, not on the explanation of how and why the event occurred. But with each new step in the evolution of the story the relative weight and interest of Julian's crime is increased and some attempt is made to supply, if not the reasons for it, at least its antecedents. This is already noticeable in the *Golden Legend*. We are not simply told, as in the original Latin text, that 'someone foretold Julian that he would kill his parents'; the prophecy assumes a significantly concrete form:[3]

Another Julyen there was that slew his father and mother by ignorance. And this man was noble and young, and gladly went for to hunt. And one time among all other he found a hart which returned toward him and said to him, 'Thou huntest me that shall slay thy

[1] The process of lengthening begins with the 'epitomes' themselves, as may be seen from a comparison of Bartholomew of Trent's collection (1244) with the *Legenda Aurea* which is at least 22 years later. For a complete list of French saints' lives in verse and prose see Paul Meyer's 'Légendes hagiographiques en français' in *Histoire littéraire de la France*, xxxiii. 337–78, 396–458.

[2] The earliest known version, that of Bartholomew of Trent, was published by M. Baudouin de Gaiffier from a manuscript in the Vatican (Barb. Lat. 2300). See his 'Légende de S. Julien l'Hospitalier' in *Analecta Bollandiana*, vol. lxiii, pp. 168–9.

[3] I am quoting from Caxton's translation of the *Golden Legend*, based not on the Latin, but on Jean de Vignay's French rendering, and yet remarkably close to the Latin original. The spelling has been modernized.

father and mother.' Hereof was he much abashed and afeard, and for dread that it should not happen[1] to him that the hart had said to him he went privily away, that no man knew thereof.

The Latin text says: 'Unde cum uxore in longinquam regionem fugit occulte.' Jacobus a Voragine gives more details:

[Julian] found a prince, noble and great, to whom he put him to service. And he proved so well in battle and in services in his palace that he was so much in the prince's grace that he made him knight and gave him a rich widow of a castle,[2] and for his dowry he received the castle.

His parents then 'put them in the way for to seek him in many places':

·And so long they went till they came to the castle where he dwelled, but then he was gone out and they found his wife. And when she saw them she enquired diligently who they were, and when they had said and recounted what was happened of their son she knew verily that they were the father and mother of her husband, and received them much charitably, and gave to them her own bed and made another for herself. And on the morn the wife of Julyen went to the church, and her husband came home while she was at church, and entered into his chamber for to awake his wife. And he saw twain in his bed, and wend that it had been a man that had laid with his wife, and slew them both with his sword.

The next scene is that of Julian's discovery of his crime, summed up by Bartholomew of Trent in one sentence: 'Dum foras aggreditur occurrit et dum se parricidam intelligit evigilans, sepellit interfectos.' Jacobus a Voragine develops this into a dialogue:

And after went out and saw his wife coming from church. Then he was much abashed and demanded of his wife who they were that lay in his bed. Then she said that they were his father and his mother which had long sought him, and she had laid them in his bed. Then he swooned, and was almost dead, and began to weep bitterly, and cry:

'Alas! caitif that I am! What shall I do that have slain my father and mother? Now it is happened, that I supposed to have eschewed!'

---

[1] = that it might happen.   [2] = who had a castle of her own.

And said to his wife,

'Adieu and farewell, my right dear love! I shall never rest till that I shall have knowledge if God will pardon and forgive me that I have done, and that I shall have worthy penance therefor.'

And she answered,

'Right dear love, God forbid that you should go without me! Like as I have had joy with you, so will I have pain and heaviness.'

The description of Julian's penance is substantially the same in both texts: Julian and his wife come to 'a great river over which much folk passed, where they edified an hospital much great for to harbour poor people and there do their penance in bearing men over that would pass'. One night, as Julian slept 'sore travailed', he heard a voice 'lamenting and crying' which said, 'Julian, come and help us over!'

And anon he arose and went over and found one almost dead for cold, and anon he took him and bore him to the fire, and did great labour to chafe and warm him. And when he saw that he could not be chafed nor warmed, he bore him into his bed and covered him the best wise he might. And anon after, he that was so sick and appeared as he had been a mesel,[1] he saw all shining ascending to heaven, and said to Saint Julian, his host:

'Julian, Our Lord hath sent me to thee, and sendeth thee word that He hath accepted thy penance.'

And a while after Saint Julian and his wife rendered unto God their souls and departed out of this world.

This version is at least eleven years later than Bartholomew of Trent's; and while it represents an important stage in the process of expansion, it clearly leaves room for more: it still takes the facts of the story for granted; everything happens, as in the original Latin 'epitome', *occulto Dei iudicio*, and the question 'why?' remains unanswered except in terms of the unfathomed designs of Providence.

An attempt to answer it in another way was made by two anonymous French writers of the thirteenth century, a poet

---

[1] = leper.

and a prose writer.[1] The contribution of the prose writer is particularly significant. Having noticed that, according to the *Golden
Legend*, Julian 'gladly went for to hunt' and that the fatal prophecy
was uttered by a hunted animal, he perceived a possible link
between the reference to hunting and the part played by the
supernatural prophecy—the two 'adventitious' features of the
Golden Legend, unknown to the original version. In an effort to
relate them to one another he said at the very outset that Julian's
passion for hunting was becoming irresistible. Julian would not
let a day pass without going into the woods with his dogs.[2]
One day, the tale goes on, Julian was out hunting, and his companions said to him that he had been out long enough, for both
men and dogs were weary. He refused to turn back and said:
'Go, leave me. I do not wish to return yet. I shall seek more
adventures in the forest.' The few men who followed him soon
found themselves far behind. Julian, left alone, came upon an
animal hidden in a deep thicket. He went round the thicket to
discover how best to take aim, but as he approached, the animal
cried out and said: 'Child, kill me not. I shall tell you your destiny.
You will, with a single stroke, kill your father and mother.'
When Julian heard this he withheld his arrow, but after a moment

---

[1] The poem was published in 1899 by Adolf Tobler, and the prose tale in 1901 by
Rudolf Tobler, both in the *Archiv für das Studium der neueren Sprachen und Littera-
turen* (cii. 109–78, cvii. 79–102). The prose version is a carefully planned and fully
articulated composition, showing distinct traces of a metrical source, but totally different in character. Rudolf Tobler thought that because the prose tale was superior
to the poem it must be earlier: 'Wie aber die Prosalegende klarer und zugleich poe-
tischer ist als die gereimte, so darf man wohl auch annehmen, daß sie der ursprüng-
lichen Form der Legende näher steht' (vol. cvi, p. 315). The underlying doctrine has
done incalculable damage to medieval literary studies both in Tobler's time and
since. Paul Meyer (op. cit., p. 388), without raising the general issue, emphatically
rejected Tobler's view and pointed out that the opening lines of the prose tale
clearly refer to a French source. The occurrence in the prose text of complete octo-
syllabic lines from the poem, which Tobler is at pains to dismiss as a mere accident,
should leave no doubt as to the priority of the metrical version. A further piece of
evidence is that the 'messenger from heaven' who appears both in the *Golden Legend*
and in the verse rendering is replaced in the prose tale by Jesus Christ. The reverse
process would be unthinkable.

[2] Vol. cvii, p. 81 (the italics are mine): '*et ama deduit de chiens et d'oisiaus sor toutes
coses*, et deduit de bois ama il tant qu'a grant paine s'en pooit il un jor soufrir ne ja
ne li anuiast. *Et il ot un jor ses chiens lassés* etli loerent si compaignon ke il s'en alast, car il lor
anuioit cascun jor par le bois. Et quant li enfes l'oï si lor dist: "Alés vos ent, car je ne
m'en irai pas encore, *ains irai querant aventure par ce bois*." *Atant a pris son arc, si s'en va*.'

again stretched his bow. The animal cried out, repeating the same words. Amazed and frightened though he was, Julian took aim, but once more the animal said: 'Child, kill me not, for I tell you truly, with one stroke you will kill your father and mother, and wherever you go no one but God can prevent this happening.' Trembling with terror, Julian smashed his bow and his arrows and said, 'Vile beast, you lie!' He swore never to go to any place where he might see his father and mother, discarded his armour, and went on a pilgrimage to Rome and the Holy Land. On his return he set out for Compostella. One day, however, he found himself in a besieged castle where the sight of a battle tempted him to resume the life from which he had fled. He forgot St. James and the pilgrimage, became a knight, and married a noble lady. His parents, who had been searching for him far and wide ever since he left them, came at last to his castle. He was away, but his wife welcomed them and gave them her own bed. And as they lay asleep in bed, Julian, not knowing that they had come, entered the darkened room, thought for a moment that a man was lying with his wife, rushed to the bed 'com hors del sens' ('as a man out of his mind'), and killed his mother and father.

How did this come about? According to the *Golden Legend*, when Julian's parents arrived he was absent 'by chance' (*casu*). He had 'gone out', says Caxton, 'and they found his wife'. The French prose tale tells us that that day he had gone out hunting. He stayed out longer than he had intended, and the disaster occurred when after a whole day and a whole night of hunting he came home, alighted from his horse, and in all haste went into the castle. This *reprise* of the theme of hunting establishes a pattern unknown to the *Golden Legend*; and the impact of the two parallel situations upon the reader's mind is such that the whole sequence of events acquires a new *kind* of coherence. Julian's love of hunting had supplied a reason for his encounter with the hunted animal and for the curse the wounded stag laid upon him: this was part of a causal sequence; but to account for a still more terrible happening—Julian's crime—what was needed was something more immediately impressive: an interplay of two parallel movements. We were told at the beginning of the story that Julian's one great passion was hunting—*deduit de chiens et de bois*: the joys of the chase —a passion so strong that he could not bear to live a single day without rushing into the woods with his companions; and we were also told that just before Julian met the animal which prophesied his crime he abruptly left his companions.[1] Both motifs are echoed almost word for word just before the scene of the murder. When Julian's mother asks what his favourite pastime is, his wife replies that his greatest joy is hunting—*deduit de chiens*;[2] and when, after a whole night and morning of hunting, Julian remembers that it is time for him to return home, he quickly abandons his companions.[3] The effect of the recurrence is to make the fulfilment of the prophecy seem imminent: on the first occasion the two motifs lead up to the prophecy, on the second they make it come true[4]—a striking example of the harnessing of the supernatural to a sense of coherence and plausibility.[5]

To most modern readers the legend of St. Julian is known through Flaubert's *Légende de saint Julien l'Hospitalier*—one of his *Trois Contes* published in 1876. The story is concluded by the remark:

Et voilà l'histoire de saint Julien l'Hospitalier, telle à peu près qu'on la trouve, sur un vitrail d'église, dans mon pays.

'Dans mon pays' means in his native city of Rouen, and the 'vitrail d'église' is one of the stained-glass windows in the north transept of Rouen cathedral. Flaubert must have known not only the

[1] 'Il se destorna d'els au plus tost qu'il pot, et quant il s'aperçut ke si compaignon l'orent perdu', etc. (loc. cit.).

[2] *Archiv für das Studium der neueren Sprachen*, p. 93: 'et ele li dist k'il n'amoit nul deduit tant come de chiens, dont il a molt grant plenté'.

[3] Ibid., p. 95: 'Maintenant laisça ses compaignons et ses chiens, [et] la plus droite voie qu'il savoit venus est en sa cort.'

[4] A similar development is suggested in the Latin *Historia beati viri Iuliani martiris*, which says that when Julian's parents came to his castle he was out hunting: 'venacionis causa silvas locaque deserta penetrabat' (see Baudoin de Gaiffier, op. cit., p. 211).

[5] The editor of the text, Rudolf Tobler, describes the action of the tale as follows: 'Das Fatum, welches in der Prosalegende waltet, ist keine willkürlich eingreifende Macht, die den Menschen schuldlos ins Verderben treibt. Es ist hier, wie schon in der antiken Ödipussage, der Charakter des Menschen, seine innere Natur, die seine Handlungen, also sein Schicksal regiert. Das ist in unserer Prosalegende konsequent durchgeführt, freilich ohne daß der Leser auf die dabei gewahrte innere Gerechtigkeit aufmerksam gemacht wird, ebensowenig übrigens, wie das in der griechischen Sage und ihren Bearbeitungen zu geschehen pflegt' (op. cit., p. 138).

window itself, but its description in a book by his art master at the Collège de Rouen, Eustache-Hyacinthe Langlois,[1] who had published in the same volume his own rendering of the story based upon the *Golden Legend*. But had this been the extent of Flaubert's knowledge of the legend it is doubtful whether he would ever have written his *conte* in the form in which we have it. Unlike the early writers of saints' lives, Flaubert was primarily concerned not with the consequences but with the antecedents of Julian's crime; what he wanted to know was not how Julian became a saint, but how he became a sinner. Although as early as 1856 there is in Flaubert's correspondence a reference to his interest in the legend,[2] it was not until the autumn of 1875, when he was staying at Concarneau, that he started to write his own version of it.[3] The work proceeded at first at an exasperatingly slow pace: half a page in a fortnight. Then for ten days there seems to have been no progress at all. 'Ce n'est pas commode à écrire, cette histoire-là,' he writes on 17 October;[4] and four days later admits that the story is not advancing much.[5] But early in November he decides to go to Paris to look at some books in the Bibliothèque Nationale, and soon after his arrival a marked change occurs in the tone of his remarks about this 'medieval trifle' ('petite bêtise moyennageuse').[6] He estimates that it will take him another two weeks to finish the first part and promises to complete the entire work by the end of February.[7] In the event he finished it even sooner, on 17 February.[8] Such evidence as

[1] *Essai historique et descriptif sur la peinture sur verre . . . et sur les vitraux les plus remarquables* (Rouen, 1832). The basic material for the following pages will be found in my essay *Flaubert and the Legend of Saint Julian* published in the *Bulletin of the John Rylands Library* in 1953 (xxxvi. 228–44), and in a typewritten thesis by Miss S. M. Smith in the Manchester University Library.

[2] Letter to Louis Bouilhet (1 June).

[3] Cf. Marie-Jeanne Durry, *Flaubert et ses projets inédits* (Paris, 1950), 367.

[4] *Correspondance, édition du centenaire*, iii. 229.

[5] Ibid., p. 230.

[6] In a letter to George Sand, *Correspondance*, p. 234.

[7] Cf. ibid., vii. 283, and the letter just quoted.

[8] On 18 February he wrote to George Sand: 'I finished my story last night.' In a letter to her dated 6 February he says that he has been doing more reading in connection with his work on the legend. Dr. Colin Duckworth in his edition of the text suggests that this was the day when Flaubert discovered one of the manuscripts of the medieval prose tale in the Bibliothèque Nationale. I would be inclined to date the finding of the text a month or two earlier.

we have suggests that this quickening of the tempo was primarily
due to a literary discovery: that of the thirteenth-century French
prose tale.[1] The spark that passed at that moment between two
kindred minds separated by the gulf of six centuries seems to
have had a decisive effect upon the shaping of Flaubert's tale.
The two movements, one leading to the encounter with the
miraculous animal, the other to the scene of the murder of Julian's
parents, reappear in his *Légende*, with a fresh emphasis upon
their contrasting features. The first movement begins quietly,
as a typical hunting scene. On a winter morning Julian sets out
before dawn, with a bow slung across his shoulder. As he enters
the forest he sees a woodcock sitting on a branch, its head beneath
its wing. With the flat of his sword he cuts off its feet and leaves
it lying on the ground. He then comes to an avenue of tall trees
where other animals begin to appear:

Un chevreuil bondit hors d'un fourré, un daim parut dans un carre-
four, un blaireau sortit d'un trou, un paon sur le gazon déploya sa
queue;—et quand il les eut tous occis, d'autres chevreuils se présen-
tèrent, d'autres daims, d'autres blaireaux, d'autres paons, et des merles,
des geais, des putois, des renards, des hérissons, des lynx, une infinité
de bêtes, à chaque pas plus nombreuses. Elles tournaient autour de lui,
tremblantes, avec un regard de supplication . . . Julien ne se fatiguait
pas de tuer . . .

The tale of the savage slaughter of wild creatures unfolds
itself like a medieval animal ornament. Suddenly an extraordinary
sight makes Julian pause. In a deep valley he sees a great herd
of deer huddled together and warming one another with their
breaths. For a few minutes he stands, breathless with joy. But
as his first arrow speeds through the air the deer turn their heads

---

[1] In the light of recent research it would appear that he must have seen both a
manuscript of the tale (probably MS. B.N. fr. 6447) and a modern adaptation of the
text by Lecointre-Dupont published in the *Mémoires de la Société des Antiquaires de
l'Ouest* (année 1838). Cf. A. W. Raitt, 'The Composition of Flaubert's *Saint Julien
l'Hospitalier*', *French Studies*, xix (1965), 358 ff. Other recent writings on the subject
include Dr. C. Duckworth's introduction and commentary to his edition (London,
1959; 2nd ed. 1963), Signor Sergio Cigada's review of this edition in *Studi francesi*
(vol. xxii, Jan.–Apr. 1964), his 'I *Trois Contes* nella storia dell'arte flaubertiana' (*Con-
tributi del Seminario di filologia moderna*, seria francese ii (Milan, 1961), 252–69), and
Dr. R. A. E. Baldick's introduction to his translation of *Trois Contes* (London, Penguin
Books, 1961).

towards him and utter plaintive cries. Then, as the arrows begin
to fall thick and fast, the animals, trapped in the enclosed valley
and maddened with terror, climb upon one another, their bodies
forming a moving mountain which finally falls apart. Julian sees
them lying dead on the ground, and as he is leaning against a
tree, wondering how he has accomplished this great slaughter,
'he sees a large stag with a doe and a fawn. . . . He stretches his
bow and instantly the fawn drops dead, and as its mother raises
her head uttering a cry of anguish Julian thrusts his knife into
her throat and fells her to the ground.' Then the great stag springs
forward. Julian aims his last arrow at him, and the shaft sticks
deep between the antlers. But the stag still advances towards
Julian as if to charge him, and Julian recoils in horror. Presently
the huge animal halts. With eyes aflame and the solemn air of
a patriarch and a judge it speaks while a bell tolls far off: 'Accursed,
accursed, accursed! One day, fierce heart, you will murder your
father and mother.' Then the great beast sinks to its knees,
closes its lids, and dies. And as we listen to the prophecy, from
the familiar setting of a medieval hunting scene we step into the
dark region where destiny at last throws off its veil.

A few pages suffice to describe Julian's wanderings, his successes
on the battlefield, and his marriage to the Emperor's daughter.
One summer evening, as he kneels to pray, he hears the bark of
a fox and a soft padding under the window. In the falling shadows
he catches a glimpse of something like the forms of animals.
The second movement of the tale then begins. Julian seizes his
bow, and again, as he walks through the forest, a great stillness
reigns everywhere. A wild boar springs from behind him and
vanishes before Julian has time to grasp his bow. At the edge of
the wood he sees a wolf pause, turn its head to look at him, and
continue on its way. Shapes begin to move in the darkness.
Panting, wild-eyed hyenas approach him, sniff at him, showing
their fangs, and as he draws his sword, disappear in a cloud of
dust. He sees fiery sparks among the branches of the forest.
Those are the eyes of wild cats, squirrels, owls, parrots,
and monkeys. He aims his arrows at them all, and the arrows
alight like butterflies on the leaves; he throws stones, and the

stones fall harmlessly to the ground. And all the beasts he had once pursued surround him, some sitting on their hindquarters, others standing at full height. Cold with terror, he takes a step forward, and they all move with him, the hyenas striding in front of him, the wolf and the wild boar at his heels, while on one side the bull swings his head and on the other the panther, arching its back, advances with long velvet-foot strides. They watch him out of the corners of their eyes, and Julian, deafened by the buzzing of insects, bruised by the tails of the birds, choked by the stench of animal breaths, walks with outstretched arms and unseeing eyes, the thirst for slaughter stirring afresh within him, a thirst which the blood of animals can no longer quench.

Only a few moments later Julian sees his father and mother stretched before him, with splashes of blood on their white skin and on the ivory crucifix which hangs in the alcove. So ends the second movement of the tale, the more terrible in its impact because of its subtle resemblance to the first. The essence of it all is the symmetrical interplay of dream and reality. Just as the stark realism of the wholesale slaughter of animals dissolves into the supernatural prophecy, so the dream-like terror of the animal world, closing in upon Julian and pursuing him as if to wreak a supernatural vengeance upon him, culminates in the tragic reality of his predestined crime. There is, of course, something else as well, something that might suggest a realistic explanation of the crime. The description of Julian's initiation into the art of hunting is lengthened and the background of his early years extended so as to provide the kind of motivation that one expects to find in a story of character and motive. There is in fact enough 'psychology' there to satisfy those who think that in art, as in real life, human behaviour can best be explained psychologically;[1]

---

[1] Some of Walter Kaufmann's remarks in his memorable essay on *Goethe versus Shakespeare* (*Partisan Review*, Nov.–Dec. 1952) would seem particularly relevant in this connection. He points out that 'the insistence on explaining all behaviour psychologically is a relatively recent development', and shows by examples from the Bible and Shakespeare how limited the relevance of such an explanation really is. Details of character may be drawn with the most admirable skill, but 'in each case the hero far surpasses any such considerations . . . Shakespeare's tragic heroes live in a world of their own, and this—no less than the witches and the ghosts—underscores the inevitability of their disaster, which is not a matter of circumstances but destiny.

certainly enough to save the appearances.[1] Julian is a medieval nobleman trained from early childhood to enjoy the most cruel of sports; and because his 'fierce heart' is the result of his up-bringing, the whole tale could, if necessary, be fitted into the familiar pattern of an action determined by psychological data which in turn are explicable in terms of certain well-defined social and historical factors. This is the way most readers interpret not only Flaubert's *Saint Julien*, but the vast narrative symphony of *Madame Bovary* and the still more complex one of *L'Éducation sentimentale*. Yet the simple facts of the history of the St. Julian legend show beyond doubt that the sense of the inevitable cannot be borne in upon the reader in so simple a fashion. Julian's seemingly natural behaviour carries conviction only when it becomes part of a movement which by its own logic brings about the tragic end. It is then that the 'secret cause' at long last becomes tangible, and as we watch the musical mode replace the rational, we discover, perhaps without even fully realizing it, the most lasting form of art yet produced by the written word.

We can observe the flowering of this same form within our modern 'poetic space' from James Joyce to T. S. Eliot, from Proust to Valéry, and beyond. For such a form naturally transcends historical boundaries and defies temporal limitations. For Thomas Mann the art of the novel was a close replica of the art of the fugue; for Dante a thing was beautiful when its parts were duly related to one another, so that we derived pleasure from their harmony: 'a song', he wrote in his *Convivio*, 'is beautiful when, in accordance with the rules of the art, its melodies answer each other'.[2] There is no need to think in this connection of a possible

---

Macbeth and Hamlet are doomed no less than Oedipus, called to do what they would rather not do, placed in a world which is not their own and among people unable to understand them.'

[1] Unfortunately, to save the appearances often means misleading the critics. Mr. Raitt (op. cit., p. 368) is still convinced that the genesis of *Saint Julien l'Hospitalier* was simply a process of 'making the story psychologically coherent by emphasizing Julian's cruelty'. Not many academic critics of today see what was already obvious to Proust and what Sergio Cigada has recently restated so well, namely that the controlling factor in Flaubert's narrative is its rhythm.

[2] *Convivio*, I. v. 13–14: 'Quella cosa dice l'uomo essere bella, cui le parti debita-mente si rispondono, per che della loro armonia resulta piacimento. Onde pare l'uomo essere bello, quando le sue membra debitamente si rispondono; e dicemo bello lo

revival of the medieval view of the art of composition.[1] What some
art historians and literary critics have taken to be a return to the
medieval concept of analogy is in reality a recurrence of one of
the constants—actual or potential—of poetic structure, occasionally
obscured by certain conventions imported from outside. Our
traditional rhetoric and the neo-classical rules of dramatic composition have at times silenced the 'melodies answering each
other'; they have never succeeded in removing such melodies
altogether from the range of our sensibility: what has in fact varied
in the course of literary history is not the degree to which analogy
has been used in prose and poetry, nor its availability to the
artist, but the degree of our comprehension of its value. And
one beneficial result of a historical inquiry such as this is to
reveal to us the unsuspected hold that such things have upon
our imagination.

canto, quando le voci di quello, secondo debito dell'arte, sono intra sè rispondenti.'
The passage has been traced through Horace to Plato, but it could just as easily have
been inspired by the Provençal and French lyrical tradition of the twelfth and thirteenth centuries. Dante's notion of voices answering each other in harmony is at one
and the same time a poetic and a musical one, since *lo canto* belongs to both arts.
The idea of *le voci* answering each other is expressed in similar terms at the end of
Paradiso 10: 'render voce a voce in tempra'. I am grateful to Professor Louis Rossi for
his help in interpreting these two passages. He writes: 'Given *Par.* 10 and 12 (12. 21:
"se l'estrema all'intima rispose") the idea of an antiphonal response would seem to be
a natural suggestion where Dante uses *voci* and *rispondere* together.'

<hr>

[1] Cf. Wilhelm Worringer, op. cit.; Joseph Frank's essay 'Spatial Form in
Modern Literature' in *The Sewanee Review* (1945), liii (nos. 2, 3, 4); and the relevant
portion of my essay on *The Historical Method in the Study of Literature* (*Acta of the
Jubilee Congress of the Modern Humanities Research Association* (Cambridge, 1969)).

VII

A NEW HORIZON

THE 'noble and joyous book' which Sir Thomas Malory concluded in the 'ninth year of the reign of King Edward IV' and which Caxton published under the title of *Le Morte Darthur* fifteen years later—in July 1485—contained a great variety of Arthurian matter, mostly drawn from the French romances of the thirteenth century; and although nearly all Malory's sources have been identified,[1] there are few more delicate tasks than that of assessing the exact extent and nature of his own contribution. It is comparatively easy to discover what it was that Malory liked or disliked in his models. On the basis of some of his deliberate omissions and alterations it can be shown, for instance, that he took a sceptical view of the supernatural and that his conception of the role and purpose of chivalry was practical rather than idealistic. But to say this is to describe him rather than the nature of his work. And because most critics tend to do precisely this, we are on the whole better informed about Malory the man and his conscious preferences than about his achievement as a writer. In Malory's version of the story of Balin, which forms part of his *Tale of King Arthur*, the first of his eight romances, there is evidence of the suppression of some of the supernatural elements;[2] but the essential magic of the tale is retained and its poetic meaning is brought home to us at least as clearly as in Malory's original. Still more significant is the case of the *Tale of the Sankgreal* or *The Quest of the Holy Grail*. Malory consistently removed the long theological commentary supplied in the French *Queste del Saint Graal* by anonymous hermits who appear at various points in the story. In the English version

---

[1] With the exception of such models as he may have had for his *Book of Sir Gareth of Orkney* and for some parts of his two Lancelot romances, the *Noble Tale of Sir Lancelot du Lake* and the *Book of Sir Lancelot and Queen Guinevere*. Cf. the relevant sections of the *Commentary* in my edition of *The Works of Sir Thomas Malory* (Oxford, 1967, 2nd edn.).

[2] Cf. my *Malory* (Oxford, 1929), 52–3; and *Essays on Malory*, ed. J. A. W. Bennett (Oxford, 1963), 11–13, 33–4.

the complex theme of Lancelot and Galahad is left to speak for itself. No comment is made to convey the sense of the divine irony whereby Lancelot's begetting of Galahad is at one and the same time a grave offence against the courtly code and, in the context of the Grail quest, Lancelot's chief *raison d'être*. But the feeling of the approaching ruin of earthly values is all the stronger for that, and the clearer the apprehension of the 'piercing moment' when, as Charles Williams has it, 'the spiritual bids its implacable farewell to the natural'. A subtle process of adaptation in which author and model play an equally vital part makes it possible for the work to be different from what any of the earlier writers had imagined, and different again from what Malory himself had consciously intended it to be. In a well-known passage C. S. Lewis compares it to a cathedral which no single man foresaw as it now is, and which occupies a position half way between the works of art and those of nature;[1] to him Malory's romances were comparable to Wells cathedral rather than to Liverpool cathedral: they were only the last phase of something at which many generations had laboured for centuries. 'Here', he wrote, 'is a Middle English crypt, there an Anglo-Norman chapel, a late French bit, and bits that are almost pure Malory.' The comparison is helpful as long as we bear in mind that 'pure Malory' means something more than what he planned, much more than what he occasionally added to the material he had inherited. 'Pure Malory' is in fact not always separable from 'Middle English crypts', 'Anglo-Norman chapels', or 'late French bits'; it is something which, even without the author's knowledge, can fulfil the apocalyptic promise: 'Behold, I make all things new.' Sometimes this undefinable element may even defeat the author's intentions and secure a victory for art over his conscious self—for the greater self over the smaller. Traditional academic criticism has so far been on the side of the vanquished and has directed its powerful techniques of inquiry towards the discovery of everything that is separable from the creative endeavour of the mind. But every now and again the voice of a critical conscience is heard, appealing for a reversal of the common trend, for an acceptance of what Gaëtan Picon describes as 'mouvement

[1] *Essays on Malory*, ed. J. A. W. Bennett, p. 28.

de la sensibilité sous l'éclair d'une révélation'—an emotion illumined
by the powers of perception and the gift of discovery.

It was Mario Praz who once said in a broadcast from Rome
Radio[1] that what from the standpoint of the earlier, cyclic romances
was corruption could be a creative innovation if viewed from
another angle.[2] He then went on to say that in Malory

episodes tend to become independent of the laws of cyclic composition and to respond to the needs of a new world—a world which is
alive and shapeless, and quite different from traditional stylized forms:
Malory's work represents precisely this transition from medieval
romance to the modern novel.[3]

The two adjectives, 'alive' ('vivo') and 'shapeless' ('amorfo'),
used with reference to two complementary aspects of the same
phenomenon, suggest a significant contrast between amorphous
reality and stylized form. The type of narrative represented by
Malory is, on this showing, a less stylized one than that of his
models; it is more concerned with patterns of human behaviour
than with patterns of composition; it favours dialogue rather
than description, and in the treatment of dialogue preserves the
eloquent abruptness of colloquial speech:

il dialogo è vivo e diretto, e può far pensare i moderni al dialogo di
Hemingway, che ha ripreso ai nostri giorni quella tecnica primitiva di
resa immediata ed economica d'una conversazione.

There are few equally apt definitions of Malory's art in recent
criticism. Comparisons with his sources may reveal passages
due to his own invention—significant disquisitions on love and
marriage,[4] examples of genuine lyricism,[5] long and elaborate
comments on the art of chivalry and the meaning of the 'High

[1] See my 'Epic and Tragic Patterns in Malory', in *Friendship's Garland: Essays
presented to Mario Praz* (Rome, 1966), i. 81 ff.
[2] 'Come tutti gli ultimi rampolli d'una tradizione, l'opera di Malory presenta
differenze che, a seconda del punto di vista, possono apparire come degenerazioni
o come innovazioni.'
[3] '. . . gli episodi tendono a rendersi independenti dalle leggi della composizione
ciclica, e ad obbedire alle sollecitazioni di un mondo nuovo, vivo, amorfo, ben diverso
dalle stilizzate forme tradizionali: l'opera di Malory rappresenta appunto questa
transizione dal romanzo medievale al romanzo moderno.'
[4] Cf. *The Works of Sir Thomas Malory*, pp. 1119–20, 1407–8.
[5] Cf. ibid., pp lxxxiii–lxxxviii.

Order of Knighthood';[1] yet the changes that help us to see most
clearly Malory's special characteristics as a writer occur in a story
in which there is little room for such digressions, *The Tale of the
Death of King Arthur*, the last and the greatest of his romances.
Here the reinterpretation is achieved by means of a subtle choice
of scenes and motifs, a skilful expansion of soliloquies and dialogues,
or through the sheer power of the words spoken by the characters.
It is probably true that if 'many generations' had not laboured
upon this theme Malory's *Tale* would not have been what it is;
but it is also true that what matters in this work is something
which had never existed before—something at one and the same
time related to the tradition that lies behind it, and unthinkable
except in terms of the reshaping of the tradition at Malory's hands.

The reason given by Caxton in his preface for the publication
of Malory's romances was that he thought it was time, as one
'noble gentleman' had told him, that someone made known 'the
history of the noble king and emperor, King Arthur', since he was
born within the realm of England and there were in French and
other foreign languages 'diverse and many volumes of his acts,
and also of his knights'.[2] Caxton was perhaps unaware that in
this way he was rescuing from oblivion not merely an English
king and conqueror, but a great English classic and the vast
tradition which through *Le Morte Darthur* was eventually trans-
mitted to the modern world.[3] Many successive writers worked on
the French Arthurian prose romances between the thirteenth
and the fifteenth centuries; there were adaptations of them in
Italy, in Spain, and in Germany; but all this is now dead and forgotten, and Malory's work alone has defied all changes of taste,

---

[1] Cf. *The Works of Sir Thomas Malory*, pp. xxix–xxxiv.

[2] 'And many noble volumes be made of hym and of his noble knyghtes in Frensshe,
which I have seen and redde beyonde the see, which been not had in our maternal
tongue. But in Walsshe ben many, and also in Frensshe, and somme in Englysshe,
but nowher nygh alle' (ibid. cxlv).

[3] Nor did he realize that for four and a half centuries he would have to stand
between Malory and his readers, admired by all for having preserved the 'noble and
joyous book', but arousing in some uneasy feelings as to how he had dealt with the
precious copy 'unto him delivered'. It was not until the discovery in 1934, in the
Fellows Library of Winchester College, of a fifteenth-century manuscript of the
work that Caxton's contribution came to be properly assessed. Cf. op. cit., introduction, 'The Story of the Book'.

style, and morals. How did this come about? It can, of course, be argued that as long as Arthur was thought to be a great English king there was room for a keen patriotic interest in the story of his reign. But looking at the Arthurian tradition from the modern angle, we are apt to forget that the French Arthurian Cycle was not essentially an epic of Arthur: it was an epic of Lancelot, and Lancelot was King of France, not of Britain.[1] If, then, all the modern French adaptors and remodellers of Arthurian romances failed so lamentably where Malory alone succeeded, the explanation should be sought in another direction.

If we placed Malory in the 'circular room' which E. M. Forster has so vividly described, he would stand at the close of one and at the opening of another vista: the traditional matter of medieval romance is still *his* world, but the form is not. He is aware of the intricacies and the dangers of his French books of chivalry, and he also knows that short of allowing knights-errant to lose all sense of direction, there are only two ways of dealing with them: one is to let them go on weaving the fabric of their adventures exactly as they did in the great Arthurian Cycle, and the other to make each knight complete any adventure he undertakes before embarking upon the next. Inevitably, Malory prefers the latter method; not only because almost any man of his time would have preferred it if faced with the same choice, but because his natural make-up is such that, like ourselves, he cannot stretch his field of vision beyond a certain range. For him the vast, slowly unrolling panorama of Arthurian chivalry is too wide to be seen as a whole. He has to single out particular sections of it if he is to grasp it at all; and this compels him occasionally to rearrange the figures moving about the landscape and by so doing shift the emphasis from one aspect of the action to another.

There is perhaps a sense in which all the fundamental changes in the form of the European novel are determined by some such variations in the range of vision—in the quantity of things that

[1] In the French 'Vulgate' Cycle the last branch known as *La Mort le Roi Artu* is concluded by the remark: 'Si se test ore atant mestre Gautiers Map de l'*Estoire de Lancelot*, car bien a tout mené a fin selonc les choses qui en advindrent, et fenist ci son livre si outreement que aprés ce n'en porroit nus riens conter qui n'en mentist de toutes choses' (ed. Jean Frappier (Paris, 1936), 238).

one can see at a glance. Our modern novel corresponds to our
present, very limited range, while the thirteenth-century cyclic
novel leaves us far behind, just as it must have left Malory and his
readers far behind. It is not a question of bulk or length, but of
arrangement. Many adaptors have tried without success to make
the Arthurian Prose Cycle accessible to the modern reader by
cutting it down, and at one time it was thought that all Malory
had done was, in Caxton's phrase, to 'reduce' his material into
English. What no other adaptor and no critic of Malory seem to
have realized is that a genuine cyclic composition could only be
modernized if the fabric of interwoven themes were carefully
unravelled and each theme placed separately upon the canvas.
If Malory had merely let this fabric shrink he would have achieved
little. What he had to do was to present each of the component
elements of the Cycle in a reduced perspective. To arrive at this
result he had to use two different techniques. Sometimes, when he
found an episode which in the original formed part of a long
recurrent theme, he tried to make it self-contained by cutting
the connecting threads. He did this with a number of incidents
in which Lancelot played the leading part, well aware though he
was that outside the complex pattern of adventures to which these
incidents belonged they could not retain their initial meaning. He
applied the same method to the story of Balin, thinking of it not
in terms of an antecedent to the story of Galahad and the Grail,
but in terms of Balin's own fate; and, as we shall see, he dealt
likewise, but even more consciously and constructively, with
the story of Arthur himself. His other technique, inspired by the
same sense of 'singleness', was more elaborate: when the strands
of a particular narrative thread could not be left as separate stories,
he joined them together end to end, so as to form an uninterrupted
sequence. His story of the *Fair Maid of Astolat* is made up of
eight such strands—eight sections which in the French source
had stood apart, interspersed with other matters.

There still remain in Malory's text many traces of the original
method of interweaving—occasional cross-links in the form of
references and allusions to what came before or to what was still
to come; but the function of such references is different from what

it was in the French romances. There they served as keystones of the entire structure; without them the work could have been neither understood nor enjoyed. They were a clear and deliberate expression of the belief that the reader liked being reminded of what he knew and that the exercise of memory was an enjoyable pursuit. Malory and, for that matter, most modern writers assume that for those who cannot remember everything there is some satisfaction in knowing that it does not really matter whether they remember it or not. What the reader and the writer lose as a result of this change of attitude is the feeling of indefinite width, the fascination of watching an expanding canvas of interwoven themes; what they gain is comparable to what medieval sculpture gained when it ceased to be an organic part of the closed universe of architectural fancy. They proclaim their independence from the rich and varied world of the cyclic narrative, even though traces of their past allegiance are visible in their contours and substance: they look back upon the old world while standing on the threshold of the new.

The earliest known account of the fall of Arthur's kingdom is contained in Geoffrey of Monmouth's *Historia Regum Britanniae* written in 1136.[1] Geoffrey describes how Arthur, having defeated the Roman army, was preparing to march into Italy; how he heard of the treachery of Mordred 'Medraut' who by force had taken his crown and married the queen; and how on his return to Britain Arthur was attacked by the rebel army. He put Mordred to flight and three days later defeated him at Winchester; but Mordred retreated to Cornwall, and the final contest took place beside the river Camel where after a long and savage battle Mordred was slain and Arthur mortally wounded. Geoffrey stresses the horror of the last battle, the fury of the onslaught and the plight of the wounded, but otherwise treats the episode with epic detachment, as a military disaster for which the chances of war were alone to blame. The same may be said of Wace's *Brut*—an adaptation of Geoffrey's *Historia* in French verse, written in 1155—and of

---

[1] In the following pages I have reproduced two extracts from my introduction to *The Tale of the Death of King Arthur* (Oxford, 1955): pp. viii–ix and xv–xvi.

8120052

its English successor, Layamon's *Brut*. Apart from the expression of indignation at Mordred's action in the opening scenes, Wace's narrative is just as bare as Geoffrey's and even more dispassionate.

It was in this form that the story reached the author of the thirteenth-century prose *Lancelot*[1]—the central branch of the Arthurian Prose Cycle. The two final sections of this romance, *La Queste del Saint Graal* and *La Mort le roi Artu*, or *La Mort Artu*, were both, in spite of their titles, primarily concerned with Lancelot. The object of the *Queste* was to show how after achieving his greatest triumphs in the world of Arthurian chivalry Lancelot failed, and how his son Galahad succeeded, in the quest of the Grail; and the object of the *Mort Artu* was to describe Lancelot's final failure: the failure to save Arthur's kingdom. And because both works were part of one romance, they were closely linked with one another: the *Queste* led up to the *Mort Artu* by condemning 'earthly' chivalry in the name of a religious ideal hitherto ignored by Lancelot; but it was also part and parcel of the entire Cycle, the purpose of which was to present the issue in contrasting terms, and so to integrate seemingly contradictory themes in a structure of the greatest possible diversity.

Lancelot, fighting to rescue Guinevere from the stake, unwittingly kills Gawain's brother, Gaheret (Malory's Gareth), and no sooner does Gawain discover this than he becomes Lancelot's mortal enemy. Lancelot is exiled to France, Arthur and Gawain follow him, besiege him in his castle, and Gawain challenges him to a single combat. Reluctantly Lancelot accepts the challenge and in the course of a fierce combat inflicts a grievous wound upon Gawain. When news is brought to Arthur of Mordred's rebellion he returns to England with Gawain and all his men, but Gawain dies of his wound soon after they land in Dover. We have seen how Arthur's subsequent defeat, left unexplained by the chroniclers, was accounted for by their successors, the French romance writers of the thirteenth century.[2] To such obvious

---

[1] He may also have known its adaptation in the prose work usually described as the *Didot-Perceval* (ed. W. Roach (Philadelphia, 1941)), but there is nothing in that work that would explain the subsequent treatment of the Death of Arthur theme in the Prose Cycle (cf. ed. cit., pp. 265–77).

[2] Cf. above, pp. 89–91.

antecedents of the disaster as the Grail story and the Lancelot–
Guinevere theme they added the Wheel of Fortune, Mordred's
incestuous birth, and the treacherous intrigues of Morgan le Fay.
Hence several narrative sequences leading up to the story of
Arthur's death.[1] Of these sequences one was of special significance
so far as Malory was concerned: that which relied for its effect
upon a conflict of loyalties inherent in the traditional doctrine
and practice of chivalry. From the standpoint of the French romance
the conflict was all the more ironical because it arose from two
inseparable and complementary aspects of the institution of
knighthood: the bond of courtly love and that of feudal allegiance.
It was *because* Lancelot was a perfect knight that he was also
a perfect lover, and to place him in the centre of a disastrous
clash between the demands of courtly service and those of feudal
loyalty was tantamount to revealing the tragic potential of human
life at its most perfect.

Such would doubtless have been the true meaning and the
central issue of the great Arthurian Cycle if it had had to be
restricted to any single theme; and it was this issue that Malory
adopted as the main theme of his own version of the Death of
Arthur story. Long before this story begins, in the first section
of the *Book of Sir Lancelot and Queen Guinevere*, when Arthur thanks
Lancelot for his 'grete travayle' in saving the queen from a horrible
and unjust punishment, Lancelot replies:

My lorde, wytte you well I ought of ryght ever to be in youre
quarell and in my ladyes the quenys quarell to do batayle, for ye ar
the man that gaff me the Hygh Order of Knyghthode, and that day
my lady, youre quene, ded me worshyp. And ellis had I bene shamed,
for that same day that ye made me knyght, thorow my hastynes I
loste my swerde, and my lady, youre quene, founde hit, and lapped hit

---

[1] These stretch far back into the early branches of the Cycle: 'Dès l'*Agravain*, des
lueurs sont donc projetées sur les événements sinistres de *la Mort Artu* sans que les
ténèbres de l'avenir soient complètement dissipées . . . On a le sentiment qu'un
ennemi s'avance à demi masqué vers les chevaliers de la Table Ronde. L'entendront-
ils approcher? Sauront-ils le reconnaître quand il les croisera? Oseront-ils le regarder
en face, vont-ils lutter ou se laisser enchaîner sans résistance? Le drame de *la Mort
Artu* est surtout là, dans la répercussion psychologique des prédictions de l'*Agravain*
et dans les feintes, le mépris, la révolte ou le désespoir des personnages qui rencontrent
leur destin' (Jean Frappier, *Étude sur la Morte le roi Artu* (Paris, 1936), 275).

in her trayne, and gave me my swerde whan I had nede thereto; and ells had I bene shamed amonge all knyghtes. And therefore, my lorde Arthure, I promysed her at that day ever to be her knyght in ryght othir in wronge.[1]

The emphasis on this one theme, which runs through the whole of Malory's account of the death of Arthur, from the denunciation of Lancelot by Agravain to 'the dolorous death and departing out of this world' of King Arthur, Guinevere, and Lancelot, is new in the English Arthurian tradition. There is no attempt to highlight it either in the alliterative *Morte Arthure* or in the stanzaic *Le Morte Arthur*. Both these poems ignore the essential continuity of the French Cycle, separate its final portion from the rest, and so leave the ending unexplained. This was one reason why Malory had to rely on the French *Mort Artu* to supply him with some means of giving the story a clear and meaningful direction. It was there that he was able to descry behind the vicissitudes which wrecked Arthur's kingdom the unresolved conflict between the heroic loyalty of man to man and the devotion of the knight-lover to his lady—the clash between the sacred ties of feudal allegiance and the romantic self-denial imposed by courtly love. Nothing more was needed to endow the tale with a profound sense of cogency. Lancelot had knighted Gareth who loved him 'more than his own kin'; and Gawain, his brother, was bound to Lancelot by ties of comradeship which had stood the hardest tests. In a scene only the barest outline of which is traceable to Malory's models, Gawain exposes the treacherous schemes of Lancelot's enemies:

My lorde Arthure, I wolde counceyle you nat to be over hasty, but that ye wolde put hit in respite, thys jougemente of my lady the quene ... For I dare sey ... my lady your quene ys to you both good and trew. And as for sir Launcelot, I dare say he woll make hit good uppon ony knyght lyvyng that woll put uppon hym vylany or shame, and in lyke wyse he woll make good for my lady the quene.[2]

---

[1] *The Works of Sir Thomas Malory* (Oxford, 1967), 1058. On the origin of this passage see ibid., p. 1599. According to the French prose *Lancelot*, it was only when Lancelot received the sword sent to him by Guinevere that he ceased to be a *vallés* and became a knight. Cf. *The Vulgate Version*, iii. 137.

[2] *Malory*, p. 1174-5.

When Arthur tells Gawain to 'make ready, for she shall have soon her judgment', 'Alas!' he says, 'that ever I should endure to see this woeful day!' And the author adds: 'So Sir Gawain turned him and wept heartily.' But Lancelot's anxiety to protect Guinevere causes him to act with such rashness as to kill Gawain's two brothers, Gaheris and Gareth, and grief turns Gawain into Lancelot's mortal enemy. When he hears that Gareth is dead and that Lancelot has killed him, he 'runs unto the king, crying and weeping', and says:

A! myne uncle, kynge Arthur! My good brother sir Gareth ys slayne, and so ys my brothir sir Gaherys, whych were two noble knyghtes . . . My kynge, my lorde, and myne uncle, . . . wyte you well, now I shall make you a promyse whych I shall holde be my knyghthode, that frome thys day forewarde I shall never fayle sir Launcelot untyll that one of us have slayne that othir. And therefore I requyre you, my lorde and kynge, dresse you unto the warre, for wyte you well, I woll be revenged uppon sir Launcelot; and therefore, as ye woll have my servyse and my love, now haste you thereto and assay youre frendis. For I promyse unto God . . . for the deth of my brothir, sir Gareth, I shall seke sir Launcelot thorowoute seven kynges realmys, but I shall sle hym, other ellis he shall sle me.[1]

The struggle then begins, and the horror of it grows each time the bond between the protagonists is made more apparent. Lancelot's behaviour—'perfect in its sad deference to an ancient loyalty'[2]—is consistent throughout: 'I require you and beseech you,' he says on the eve of a battle, 'since that I am thus required and conjured to ride into the field, that neither you, my lord King Arthur, nor you, Sir Gawain, come not into the field'; and when Arthur and Gawain with sixty thousand men follow him over the seas to 'war upon his lands', he offers them peace. As the message is delivered in his name tears 'run out of the king's eyes'. But Gawain will not be reconciled; he besieges Lancelot in the city of Benwick until Lancelot, stung by his insults, is 'driven thereto as beast till a bay'. When he is forced to throw Gawain

[1] Ibid., pp. 1185–6.
[2] E. K. Chambers, *Sir Thomas Malory* (The English Association, Pamphlet no. 51, 1922), 11.

from his horse and wound him, he refuses to take Gawain's life: 'to smite a wounded man that may not stand, God defend me from such a shame!'[1] But the harm is done. While the siege goes on Mordred raises rebellion, and as Arthur lands in Dover and prepares to pursue the rebel army, Gawain dies of the wound given him by Lancelot, repenting on his death-bed of his 'hastiness and wilfulness': 'for I was this day hurt and smitten upon mine old wound that Sir Lancelot gave me. . . . And through me and my pride you have all this shame and disease, for had that noble knight, Sir Lancelot, been with you, as he was and would have been, this unhappy war had never been begun.'[2] When, on his return to England, Lancelot sees Gawain's tomb he weeps heartily and asks the people to pray 'for the soul of Sir Gawain'.[3] Seven years later, when Arthur's fellowship and the Round Table have become a mere memory, he makes the journey from Glastonbury to Amesbury only to find that Guinevere is dead. 'He wept not greatly, but sighed.' And with 'a hundred torches ever brenning about the corpse of the queen' he returns to Glastonbury, there to bury her and mourn her death, 'remembering of her beauty and of her noblesse'.[4] These two scenes, unknown in the earlier Arthurian tradition, fully bring out Malory's own understanding of the tragedy of Lancelot. Gawain and Guinevere are the symbols of Lancelot's dual allegiance, and his prayer for Gawain's soul is as much an illustration of this theme as the passage describing how he came to bury Guinevere. When she was 'put in the earth, Sir Lancelot swooned and lay long still'. To the hermit who reproved him for displeasing God he replied:

Truly . . . I trust I do not dysplease God, for He knoweth myn entente: for my sorow was not, nor is not, for ony rejoysyng of synne, but my sorow may never have ende. For whan I remembre of hir beaulté and of hir noblesse, that was bothe wyth hyr kyng and wyth hyr, so whan I sawe his corps and hir corps so lye togyders, truly myn herte wold not serve to susteyne my careful body. Also whan I remembre me how by my defaute and myn orgule and my pryde that they were bothe layed ful lowe, that were pereles that ever was lyvyng

---

[1] *Malory*, p. 1221.   [2] Ibid., p. 1230.   [3] Ibid., p. 1250.
[4] Ibid., p. 1256.

of Cristen people, wyt you wel, sayd syr Launcelot, this remembred, of their kyndenes and myn unkyndenes, sanke so to myn herte that I myght not susteyne myself.[1]

In the *Mort Artu* and in the English *Le Morte Arthur* Lancelot dies of an illness caused by the privations he has endured as a hermit; in Malory he dies because in his grief he refuses food and drink and lies day and night 'grovelling on the tomb of King Arthur and Queen Guinevere' as a loyal knight: 'and no comfort that the bishop nor Sir Bors nor none of his fellows could make him, it availed not.'

There is nothing to suggest that either the doctrine of the Grail or that of the Wheel of Fortune was in Malory's mind when he wrote this 'most piteous tale'. He says as little as he can about Arthur's prophetic dream in which the Wheel appears, and refrains from explaining the symbolism of the vision. As for the Grail, the only reference to it occurs after the disaster, when Lancelot sees Guinevere for the last time and she tells him that she cannot believe he will ever retire from the world. He replies that she has no reason to doubt his word since in the quest of the Grail he would gladly have 'forsaken the vanities of the world' but for her love ('had nat youre love bene'): 'And if I had done so at that time with my heart, will and thought, I had passed all the knights that ever were in the Sankgreall except Sir Galahad, my son.'[2] The very nature of the sentiment behind the events has clearly undergone an important change. Lancelot in Malory lives and dies as Guinevere's faithful lover; his repentance is of the grief he caused her, not of the sin he committed for her sake. And since the laws of chivalry as Malory understands them do not call for the punishment of those who have failed in the holy quest, Lancelot's chivalry remains throughout an example of moral greatness. His failure in the Grail quest, instead of condemning his love in his own eyes, demonstrates its power; it is a measure, not of his sinful life, but of his fidelity and truthfulness. This it was that made it possible for Malory to treat his Death of Arthur story as something distinct from the moral complexities which cut across

[1] Loc. cit. Malory adds 'So the Frensshe book maketh mencyon' and so conceals his departure from the source. [2] *Malory*, p. 1253.

the main body of the French Arthurian Cycle. At the end of his *Book of Lancelot and Guinevere*, immediately before embarking upon the *Tale of the Death of King Arthur*, he wrote: 'And so I leave here of this tale and overleap great books of Sir Lancelot . . . and here I go unto the *Morte Arthur*.'[1] With these words he set a new and unfamiliar scene: 'It befell in the month of May a great anger and unhap that stinted not till the flower of chivalry of all the world was destroyed and slain.'[2] Ominous shadows begin to fall on the peaceful landscape of the realm of Logres; jousts and tournaments, wanderings through mysterious forests, and encounters with imaginary enemies recede into the background, and as we lose sight of the 'true matter' of romance, we step into a reality divorced from all doctrinal background, unrelieved by any thought of eventual comfort and reward. 'Comfort thyself', Arthur says to Bedwere, 'and do as well as thou mayst, for in me is no trust to trust in. For I must into the Vale of Avalon to heal me of my grievous wound.'[3] But there is no truth even in the belief in his return to life. 'I will not say', Malory says, 'that it shall be so.'[4] And as night falls on Salisbury Plain nothing remains but the horror of the final disaster and the certainty of loss.

There is more in all this than the pathos of disaster, more even than the beginnings of realistic motivation through character. The change from the cyclic romance to a narrative intelligible without reference to anything that lies beyond it and unrelated to any wider scheme of things brings with it a new sense of the tragic; the very restriction of the field of vision heralds the advent of tragedy as an essentially modern form. The cyclic conception was one which inevitably opened up a wide perspective, be it that of earthly and divine chivalry in the Arthurian Cycle or that of Apollo's world in the *Oresteia*. Just as Orestes as seen by Aeschylus is the occasion of a conflict between certain moral powers of the Universe, so in the French Cycle Lancelot is the occasion of a conflict of powers inherent in the structure of the feudal world. Both characters enact an all-embracing moral theme, or a complex

[1] *Malory*, p. 1154.   [2] Ibid., p. 1161.   [3] Ibid., p. 1240.
[4] Ibid., p. 1242: '. . . men say that he shall com agayne, and he shall wynne the Holy Crosse. Yet I woll nat say that hit shall be so, but rather I wolde sey: here in thys worlde he chaunged hys lyff.'

of themes, to be resolved at a higher level than that of their existence, and the resolution remains in both cases the dominating interest—'a moral and intellectual rather than a tragic interest'.[1] When in the *Eumenides* Apollo promises Orestes deliverance and himself assumes responsibility for what Orestes has done, we feel the assurance that even though the Furies may pursue Orestes, the end will be peace. The eternal order of things after being disturbed will be restored and holy calm re-established. Lancelot's death in the French *Mort Artu* is likewise heralded by a vision of heavenly calm and joy: 'I had such joy,' the archbishop says to Bors, 'and was in a company of angels, greater than any gathering of people I had ever seen; and they carried the soul of our brother Lancelot to Heaven.'[2] And when he goes to Lancelot's bed and sees that his soul has departed, he gives thanks to God: 'Oh God,' he says, 'blessed be Thy name! Now verily do I know that I saw the angels make great rejoicings for him. Therefore am I sure that penitence is above all other things.'[3]

It is only in Malory that this scene becomes one of unrelieved sorrow: 'He lay as he had smiled, and the sweetest savour about him that ever they felt. Then was there weeping and wringing of hands, and the greatest dole they made that ever made man.' And instead of the archbishop's prayer of thanksgiving the conclusion comes in the form of a threnody uttered from the depths of his despair by Lancelot's brother, Sir Ector, who, when he saw Lancelot dead, 'threw his shield, sword and helm from him, and when he beheld Sir Lancelot's visage he fell down in a swoon. And when he waked, it were hard any tongue to tell the doleful complaints that he made for his brother.'[4] In this last vision of Arthurian chivalry nothing is left but the memory of the man who died in sorrow, 'the truest friend to his lover that ever bestrode horse, the truest lover, of a sinful man, that ever loved

---

[1] H. F. D. Kitto, *Greek Tragedy* (London, 1939), 59.
[2] *La Mort le Roi Artu*, ed. J. Frappier, p. 236: 'J'estoie en si grant joie et en si grant compaignie d'angres qu'onques ne vi autant de gent en leu ou ge fusse, et enportoient lasus el ciel l'ame de nostre frere Lancelot.'
[3] Ibid.: 'Ha Diex, fet li arcevesques, beneoiz soiez vos! Or sei ge veraiement que de l'ame de cestui fesoient ore li angre feste si grant com ge vi; or sei ge bien que penitance vaut seur toutes choses.'
[4] *Malory*, p. 1259.

woman, the kindest man that ever struck with sword'. And 'there was weeping and dolour out of measure'. As there was no comfort for Lancelot and Arthur in their last hour, so there is none for those who are left to lament them. Crystallized into single characters, the vast epic becomes the story of men set apart as bearers of a tragic fate, and as the circle of destiny closes in upon them, our own vision is both narrowed and intensified in the unfolding of what has come to pass. What Sir Philip Sidney said of Chaucer is equally true of the author of this tale: we are left to wonder 'whether to marvel more, either that he in that misty time could see so clearly or that we in this clear age walk so stumblingly after him.'

With Malory this adventurous voyage comes to an end, at least for the present, and with it the search for the early foundations of the most elusive of literary forms. The voyage has taken us far into the past—a past that can only be understood as part of a complex historical process, not always amenable to a strict chronological sequence. The novel as we know it today, with all the variations and apparent contradictions that the term connotes, begins at a well-defined point with the intrusion of meaning upon matter and the enrichment of the narrative by a newly discovered harmonic texture. From that moment onwards it grows in concentric circles, never losing what it has once acquired. The dual structure of twelfth-century romances, the institution of two degrees of coherence or, as some would say, of two levels of meaning, is an inducement either to integrate them or, on the contrary, to reap the full benefit of their contrast. The latter temptation is the mainspring of 'romance' in the modern sense, while the former produces the complex moving tapestry of interlocked themes, a structure which reaches its acme in the prose fiction of the last three centuries of the Middle Ages. The inevitable disintegration of this form of fiction determines in its turn the character of its converse—the compact and transparent short novel such as Malory's Death of Arthur. And over and above all this, embracing it as the outer circle embraces the inner ones, the technique of emotional progression through analogy remains as much of a constant as the cognate device in visual arts and in music. Recognizable though all these trends are in the novel of modern times, they cannot be perceived through the medium of any single 'theory'; they are all living phenomena which no general formula can adequately describe. All that remains constant throughout is the shaping genius itself and its impact upon minds attuned to its various forms of expression. The old pioneer in John Steinbeck's *Leader of the People* sums it all up by saying: 'I tell those old stories, but they're not what I want to tell. I only know how I want people to feel when I tell them.' The knowledge and the feeling survive the modes through which they speak. In silent triumph over Time, elusive and all-pervading, they live on, like Nature in Spenser's phrase, 'unseen of any, yet of all beheld'.

APPENDIX

ILLUSTRATIVE EXTRACTS FROM CRITICAL WORKS

I. Ernst Robert Curtius, *Europäische Literatur und lateinisches Mittelalter* (Bern, 1948); English translation by Willard R. Trask (Bollingen Series XXXVI: *European Literature and the Latin Middle Ages*). The following extracts from the 'Epilogue' (pp. 384–8) have a special bearing on the problem discussed in Chapter II above (pp. 17–22):

The rich development of French poetry in the eleventh, twelfth, and thirteenth centuries stands in close relationship to the contemporary Latin poetry and poetics which flourished in France and in French England . . . Because France was the pillar of *studium*; because the *artes*, with grammar and rhetoric in the lead, had their headquarters there —that is why the flower of vernacular poetry first blooms in France. . . . The question 'Why does Italian literature begin so late?' is wrongly put. The question to ask is, 'Why does French literature begin so early?' We believe that we have given the answer. But there is another question which needs to be asked: 'Why did the Latin Renaissance (1066–1230) occur only in France and Gallicized England?' Because Charlemagne's reform of education laid a foundation which was able to survive the convulsions of the ninth and tenth centuries (*note*: crisis of the Empire under Louis the Pious; the Normans before Paris, 885–7; the Saracens in the south; fall of the West Frankish Carolingians, etc.). The intellectual leadership which Germany held under the Ottos could not be maintained.
. . . It was political forces, it was the will of a great ruler, which transplanted the *studium* to France. But perhaps it could develop so brilliantly there only because Gallo-Roman taste for elaborate discourse met with the solid discipline of English schooling.

II. H. H. Glunz, *Die Literarästhetik des europäischen Mittelalters* (Bochum, 1937), 569–70:

Die Annahme, daß Dichten das Schaffen eines Organismus sei, wobei die innere Schau des Dichters sich mit der vorhandenen Materie der Sprache verbinde, ist eine Metapher und eine Erkenntnis der modernen Poetik. Das 16. Jahrhundert bekannte sie zuerst, und seither ist sie, obwohl sie mannigfachem Wechsel, veranlaßt durch den Wechsel im Glauben und in der Haltung der Dichter, unterworfen war, ihrer Struktur nach die gleiche geblieben. So wenig es erlaubt ist, sie dem Mittelalter zuzuschreiben, so wenig kann man mit den wenig tiefen literarischen Kategorien des 19. Jahrhunderts das Dichten des Mittelalters einfangen oder verstehen wollen. Die Folge der Abenteuer, die bunte Reihe von Geschichten, die keltische oder östliche Erzählung, das Herausbreiten eines Charakters, die Motivation und den Aufbau des Geschehens allein zu untersuchen auf eine Antwort auf die Frage nach dem Wollen mittelalterischer Dichter hin, heißt die Denkkategorien des neueren Kritikers der Vergangenheit aufzwingen. Von dem wahren Streben und Glauben der mittelalterischen Poeten erfährt man so nichts.

III. Fourquet, Jean, 'Le rapport entre l'œuvre et la source chez Chrétien de Troyes et le problème des sources bretonnes', '*Romance Philology*, ix (1955–6), 298–312. The following passages contain the substance of M. Fourquet's views (pp. 298–312):

(*a*) Les principes d'identité et de non-contradiction n'existent pour ainsi dire pas ici: un objet a DEUX existences, parce qu'il est engagé dans deux réseaux de relations, celles du plan chevaleresque et celles du plan mythique, qui co-existent sous le couvert du même schéma, de la même SÉQUENCE épique.

Ce qui est remarquable, c'est qu'un artiste comme Chrétien laisse transparaître, en quelque sorte en filigrane, le plan mythique. On concevrait que la motivation courtoise ait été poussée jusqu'au bout, et que tout élément mythique ait été éliminé . . .

Chrétien semble, lui, avoir consciemment évité de pousser jusqu'au bout ce que l'on a appelé la RATIONALISATION, c'est-à-dire l'effacement de la cohérence du plan mythique. Il semble qu'il apprécie le pouvoir qu'exerce sur l'auditeur un détail merveilleux comme la muraille d'air, un détail cruel comme les têtes fichées sur les pieux. L'explication humaine (par la promesse faite à la demoiselle) ne vient qu'À LA FIN: longtemps l'imagination du public est sollicitée par la même attente de l'Aventure que s'il écoutait un conte de fées. La double cohérence concilie le charme du conte ('si Peau d'Âne m'était conté, j'y prendrais un plaisir extrême', dit La Fontaine) et la fonction

de la littérature chevaleresque, qui est de présenter au monde courtois une image idéalisée de ses vertus, d'être 'édifiante' au sens de
l'éthique courtoise.

(*b*) Les oppositions entre 'celtistes' et 'anticeltistes' nous paraissent
avoir été exaspérées par la conviction COMMUNE AUX DEUX PARTIS
qu'un roman comme ceux de Chrétien devait avoir une cohérence
UNIQUE ET ESSENTIELLE qu'il fallait retrouver en dépit de tous les
accidents. . . . La solution que nous proposons est fondée sur la DUA-
LITÉ ESSENTIELLE de la genèse des œuvres de Chrétien; d'une part une
cohérence résultant d'une thèse chevaleresque, cohérence qui ne
remonte pas au delà de la création de l'œuvre par Chrétien; d'autre
part une cohérence héritée de la matière dont il s'est servi pour donner
un 'corps épique' à ses thèses, les incarner littérairement. Cette seconde
cohérence pose effectivement des problèmes qui appellent une explication historique, par une TRADITION, une continuité de transmission,
et justifient l'emploi de la méthode comparative. . . .

Ce qui a dominé jusqu'à présent, c'est la recherche des RAPPROCHE-
MENTS, qui est le premier stade de toute étude comparative; à ce
premier stade l'attitude du chercheur est pour ainsi dire ACHRO-
NIQUE: elle consiste à apercevoir des identités en interrogeant des
témoins, indépendamment de leur position dans le temps. . . . Il faut
aujourd'hui concevoir les conditions RÉELLES de transmission, se
poser des problèmes d'ÉCHELONNEMENT dans le temps, aussi bien
du côté de la tradition celtique que du côté de la tradition romane.

IV. Hermann Suchier und Adolf Birch-Hirschfeld, *Geschichte der
französischen Literatur von den ältesten Zeiten bis zur Gegenwart*
(Leipzig and Vienna, 1900), Bd. I: *Von der Urzeit bis zum 16.
Jahrhundert*, von Hermann Suchier, p. 112:

Von Berols Werk haben wir nur noch ein längeres Bruchstück, das
bis zu einem bestimmten Punkte mit Eilharts Darstellung zusam-
mengeht; dann aber hört jede Übereinstimmung auf. Dieser Sachver-
halt dürfte folgenden Grund haben. Der Liebestrank, den Tristan und
Isolde trinken, ist hier nicht, wie in den späteren Erzählungen, von
unumschränkter, sondern von zeitlich begrenzter Wirkung: sie
dauert bei Eilhart vier, bei Berol drei Jahre, um dann zu erlöschen.
Mit diesem Erlöschen des Minnezaubers, also mit der Rückgabe der
Isolt und Rückkehr Tristans, wird der älteste 'Tristan' seinen
Abschluß gefunden haben. Wenn Eilhart und Berol gerade bis zu

diesem Punkte zusammengehen und dann mit Abenteuern der Lie-
benden fortfahren, die in beiden Texten ganz verschieden sind, so
erklärt sich das am natürlichsten aus der Annahme, daß dem ältesten
'Tristan' zwei voneinander unabhängige Fortsetzungen angehängt
worden sind.

Cf. Joseph Bédier's objections to this view:[1]

Il est bien malaisé de se représenter un poème ancien qui aurait
conclu la merveilleuse histoire par un retour d'Iseut au foyer conjugal.
Désormais Iseut repentie filera donc sa quenouille auprès de son mari?
Sans doute de son côté, Tristan fondera quelque part un foyer ver-
tueux? Et Marc sera ridicule, certes, mais non le plus ridicule des trois.
... Mais, si l'on tient ces considérations pour suspectes, comme étant
des raisons de goût et de sentiment, voici un argument de fait. Si le
conteur primitif, comme le croit M. Suchier, entendait terminer son
poème à la scène de Gué aventureux, pourquoi, en cette scène finale
des adieux sans retour, a-t-il annoncé et comme amorcé des récits
ultérieurs? Béroul annonce (v. 2819) que Tristan se tiendra caché dans
la cabane du forestier Orri: à quoi bon, si le roman doit se clore aussitôt
par une réconciliation générale? Iseut donne à son ami un anneau de
jaspe vert et par deux fois (v. 2709 ss. et v. 2800 ss.) elle lui jure que,
dès qu'elle reverra cet anneau,

> Ne tor, ne mur, ne fort chastel
> Ne la tendra ne face errant
> Le mandement de son amant.

Pourquoi ce don, pourquoi ce serment, si Tristan ne doit plus lui
envoyer nul mandement, et si jamais le poète n'entend se servir de
cet anneau de jaspe vert? Il faudrait admettre que toutes ces amorces
de récits prochains sont des interpolations du continuateur. Ce n'est
pas impossible, certes, mais la vérité est autre, croyons-nous.

The truth, according to Bédier, is that it is impossible
to credit the poet of genius to whom we owe the earliest
Tristan romance with the idea of limiting the efficacy of the
potion to three or four years. Hence the assumption of a common
source (*y*) of Béroul and Eilhart, a poem derived from the *archétype*,
but introducing the limitation which enables the lovers to separate.

[1] *Le Roman de Tristan par Thomas*, ii. 237-8.

There are serious difficulties about the idea of an early Tristan poem ending with Iseult's return to Mark, but otherwise Suchier's view of the love-potion theme can be said to have prevailed. The authenticity of the Béroul–Eilhart version is no longer in doubt.

V. C. S. Lewis, *Allegory of Love* (Oxford, 1936), 300–1:

Boiardo's method is that of an interlocked story. The formula is to take any number of chivalrous romances and arrange such a series of coincidences that they interrupt one another every few pages. The English reader will be apt to think of Malory or Spenser. But Malory so often leaves his separate stories unfinished or else, if he finishes them, fails to interlock them at all (so that they drop away from the rest of the book as independent organisms) and is so generally confused that he is not a good parallel. Boiardo keeps his head: we have no doubt that if he had finished the poem all the threads would have been neatly tied up. Spenser, on the other hand, has so few stories compared with the Italian . . . and is so leisurely that he can give no idea of Boiardo's *scherzo*. Boiardo would have told the story of Spenser's first canto in a few stanzas—the story of the whole *Faerie Queene* in a few cantos. The speed, the pell-mell of episodes, the crazy carnival jollity of Boiardo are his very essence. He invents a world in which, though love and war are almost the sole occupations, yet a major character hardly ever has time to lose a life or a maidenhead, for always, at the critical moment, a strange knight, a swift ship, a bandersnatch or a boojum, breaks in, and we are caught up into another story. It is extremely enjoyable, but in a breathless way; it is rather like a ride on a switchback.

VI. [John Hughes], *The Works of Mr Edmund Spencer in Six Volumes published by Mr Hughes*, vol. i: *Remarks on the Fairy Queen*, pp. lx–lxi:[1]

These are the most obvious Defects in the Fable of the *Fairy Queen*. The want of Unity in the Story makes it difficult for the Reader to carry it in his Mind, and distracts too much his Attention to the several Parts of it; and indeed the whole Frame of it wou'd appear monstrous, if it were to be examin'd by the Rules of Epick Poetry, as they have been drawn from the Practice of *Homer* and *Virgil*. But as it is plain the Author never design'd it by those Rules, I think it

[1] John Hughes (1677–1720) published this edition in 1715.

ought rather to be consider'd as a Poem of a particular kind, describing in a Series of Allegorical Adventures or Episodes the most noted Virtues and Vices: to compare it therefore with the Models of Antiquity, wou'd be like drawing a Parallel between the *Roman* and the *Gothick* Architecture. In the first there is doubtless a more natural Grandeur and Simplicity: in the latter, we find great Mixtures of Beauty and Barbarism, yet assisted by the Invention of a Variety of inferior Ornaments; and tho the former is more majestick in the whole, the latter may be very surprizing and agreeable in its Parts.

It may seem strange indeed, since *Spenser* appears to have been well acquainted with the best Writers of Antiquity, that he has not imitated them in the Structure of his Story. Two Reasons may be given for this: The first is, That at the time when he wrote, the *Italian* Poets, whom he has chiefly imitated, and who were the first Revivers of this Art among the Moderns, were in the highest vogue, and were universally read and admir'd. But the chief Reason was probably, that he chose to frame his Fable after a Model which might give the greatest Scope to that Range of Fancy which was so remarkably his Talent. There is a Bent in Nature, which is apt to determine Men that particular way in which they are most capable of excelling; and tho it is certain he might have form'd a better Plan, it is to be question'd whether he cou'd have executed any other so well.

INDEX

Figures other than those introduced by the letter n (= footnote) refer to pages. No reference is made to footnotes in the case of items found on the same page in the body of the text.

Évolution du roman arthurien vers la fin du moyen âge, L' (by C. E. Pickford), 95 n. 5
Ewert, Alfred, 45 n. 2
Excalibur, 84–5, 87–8, 90–1, 103–4, 105, 106–7
Exegesis (biblical), 17–18, 20–1

Faerie Queene, The, 33, 53, 93, 145–6
Fair Maid of Astolat, The (by Sir Thomas Malory), 128
Fairy mistress 40; fairy tale, 33, 94
Faral, Edmond, 15 n. 2, 75 nn. 4 and 5, 89 n. 1, 102 n. 1
Fata Morgana, 86
Fénice, 25, 27, 30
Ferrier, Janet M., 95 n. 2
Feudal allegiance, 47–8, 131
Fisher King, 42, 57
Flaubert, Gustave, 12, 116–21
Florio, 70
Focillon, Henri, 77 n. 2, 78, 97 n. 5
Foerster, Wendelin, 35, 37 nn. 1 and 3
Forerunners of the French Novel (by Janet M. Ferrier), 95 n. 2
Form and Meaning in Medieval Romance, 71 n. 2
Form in Gothic (by Wilhelm Worringer), 30 n. 4, 77 n. 2, 78 n. 1, 122 n. 1
Forster, E. M., vii, 12, 51, 99, 127
Fourquet, Jean, 38 n. 1, 42, 43, 44, 54 n. 3, 142–3
Fourrier, Anthime, 25 n. 1
Fox, Charles, 94 n. 1
France, vii, 6, 33, 95, 127, 130, 141
Frank, Joseph, 122 n. 1
Frappier, Jean, 54 n. 1, 85 n. 1, 89 n. 3, 127 n. 1, 131 n. 1, 137 n. 2
Frazer, James, 53
French lyrical tradition, 121 n. 2
Friendship's Garland: Essays presented to Mario Praz, 125 n. 1
From Ritual to Romance (by Jessie Weston), 56
Frye, Northrop, 12, 15 n. 1, 31 n. 1
Fugue, 121

Gabriel, Archangel, 9
Gaheret (Gareth), 84, 130, 131, 132, 133
Gaheris (Gaherys), 133
Gaiffier, *see* Baudouin de Gaiffier
Galaad, Galahad, 51, 59–61, 64–5, 100, 124, 128, 130

Galehaut, 83
Gallo-Roman tradition of oratory, 141
Ganelon, 8, 13
Gardner, E. G., 60
Gareth, *see* Gaheret *and Book of Sir Gareth of Orkney*
Garlan, the red-haired knight, 60, 108
Garland, *see* John Garland
Gaudon, Jean, 98 n. 2
Gautier (Walter) de Châtillon, 18, 19 n. 1
Gautier (Walter), Map, 127 n. 1
Gauvain, Gawain, 53, 57, 58, 80 n. 2, 84–5, 102, 103–4, 107–9, 131–4
Genoa cathedral, 54
Geoffrey of Monmouth, 1, 55, 89, 102, 129–30, 130–4
Geoffrey of Vinsauf, 75
Geometric pattern, 79
Germany, 126
Geschichte der französischen Literatur (by Hermann Suchier and Adolf Birch-Hirschfeld), 143
Geste des révoltés, La, 47
Gilbert, Alan, 93 n. 3
Gilson, Étienne, 101 n. 1
Girart de Roussillon, 48
Girart de Roussillon (chanson de geste), 47, 48 n. 3
Girart de Roussillon and the Tristan poems (by E. S. Murrell), 47 n. 1
Giraudoux, Jean, 56
Glastonbury, 135
Glunz, H. H., 46 n. 2, 141–2
Godefroy, 35 n. 2, 36 n. 1
Goethe, viii, 66, 120 n. 1
Golden Legend, The (Legenda Aurea), 110, 111–13, 114, 115, 117
Golther, Wolfgang, 46 n. 1
Gonnot, *see* Michel Gonnot
Gorgias, 74, 85
Gormond et Isembart (chanson de geste), 47
Gothic architecture, 146
Gothic Architecture and Scholasticism (by Erwin Panofsky), 23 n. 1
Gothic sculpture, 97, 129
Gottfried von Strassburg, 15–16, 17, 21 n., 32 n. 1
Graal, *see* Grail
Graesse, Johann, 110 n. 2
Grail, Holy Grail, 50, 55, 57 n. 5, 62, 90, 124, 130, 131, 135. See also *Quest of the Holy Grail, Queste del Saint Graal*, and *Conte del Graal*